Healthy Wealth
Empowering Self Reliance
Raising Self-Esteem

Successful Investing

Using Real Estate, Stocks and Bonds

Don Chambers, CPA, MBA, PFP

Successful Investing

Using Real Estate, Stocks and Bonds

ISBN # 0-9722071-3-9

Note: Successful Investing contains the opinions, thoughts, and ideas by the author. It is sold with the understanding that the publisher is not engaged in rendering professional services. If professional advice or other expert assistance is required, the

Table of Contents

Don Chambers, is currently the president of *Healthy Wealth*, with offices located in Wailea, Hawaii and Salt Lake City, Utah. Healthy Wealth specializes in empowering individuals, families and young adults through self-reliance and financial success.

Don received his MBA from the University of Southern California, with a minor in Quantitative Methods in 1977. He also holds two undergraduate degrees, the first in Business Administration and the second in Economics. He became a CPA while working for one of the big-4 accounting firms. Don also held a California Real Estate Broker's license for many years. He earned the professional designation of Personal Financial Planner, PFP, from the University of California in 1986.

Don Chambers was one of the four original founders of Mercer Global Advisors headquartered in Santa Barbara, California. At MGA, one of the largest independent financial advisors in the U.S., Don Chambers served as the Chief Financial Officer, Treasurer and Senior Financial Planner, and was also a key member of MGA's investment committee. In 1999, when Mr. Chambers sold his interests in the company, MGA had 1.9 billion dollars of assets under management. MGA is still headquartered in Santa Barbara, California.

Don's first book *"Source Book to Economic Freedom"*, was later rewritten and appeared under the title *"Road to Economic Freedom"*. The book ran into five editions and had over 60,000 copies distributed. This book is a major rewrite of the investment portion of that work.

Don has written many articles that have been published nationwide and has also created a nationally acclaimed financial planning software program called Economic Freedom Analysis®, a registered trademark of Mercer Global Advisors. Mr. Chambers has been a respected influence in the fields of financial planning, investment management, business counseling and multigenerational wealth issues. He has lectured throughout the United States on financial planning and investing, and has been a teacher to other financial planners. He has been quoted by Money, Fortune, Morningstar, and Financial Planning magazines. He appeared on the May, 1997 cover of Barron's magazine, and was featured in an article about the top financial planners in America.

Don Chambers has committed his professional life to helping others deal successfully with money and through his education, business expertise, and life experience, brings a fresh and enthusiastic flavor to teaching others to invest successfully.

Foreword

Investing is both a "Science" and an "Art". The "art of investing", the creative side, and the "science of investing", the information side, makes investing a challenging endeavor. In this book, my hope and effort is to assist you in acquiring valuable information to make your investment journey a successful and enjoyable one.

The science of investing, which is based on access to valuable information, is quite young. The computer age, which began in the 1970s, has given us vast amounts of data. This has dramatically changed the investment world. It is important to remember we live in the short and medium term and it is impossible to really know how the future will relate to the past. Asset class relationships are stable over 25 or more years and unpredictable in the short to medium term. There are wealth creation strategies that can make the short and medium term more reliable while still maximizing long term returns. In this book, I will share these strategies with you.

The purpose of investing is to increase spendable and stored wealth. I look at this like building up your economic battery, or in other words, stored energy that can be exchanged in the market place for whatever we desire over time. Thus, you are building up your equity.

Equity is created in two basic ways. Firstly, through savings that are invested and secondly through equity building in asset ownership, such as a business interest or property owned. The initial savings or equity contribution is then grown at some rate until sold. Along the way the savings provide financial peace of mind and develop your financial management skills.

This book will help you understand how to save and how to build equity. It will then teach you how to succeed in investing by showing you how to build a well balanced long term investment strategy. I will also explore what it takes to develop the confidence to stay with that strategy in challenging times.

You will learn how to incorporate real estate into your investment strategy and I will explain how collectibles have market inefficiencies and how you can profit from these inefficiencies while having fun along the way. I will help you identify your preferred wealth building strategy. Not everyone is a good saver and not everyone is good at business or real estate equity building. It is important to understand how you are most likely to succeed with wealth creation and then direct a major portion of your energy toward that approach.

Chapter 1 - Time & Money

Compound Interest

Compound interest is the growth of capital at a steady rate over long periods of time. Compound interest can be a difficult concept. When one is first exposed to the geometric progression of numbers over time the outcome seems too good to be true. I find this concept fascinating and I hope that you will too.

When you look at a chart depicting the steady growth of an asset over a long period of time, say 40 or more years, the initial years seem so simple and the out years seem so unbelievable. The more you study what is going on the more you realize that the later years are not possible without the early years. This then begs the question, "Are the early boring years of a geometric progression really where the action is? And if that is true how come the early years look so calm and the out years look so outrageous?"

Let's say, in golf you have two 9 hole events, an early part and a later part if you will. Let's say we decide to bet 10 cents on the first hole and then double the bet every hole thereafter. On the second hole we play for 20 cents. Most people, when they study this chart, find the first column very mundane and the second column, well...outrageous! Note, however, that you could not get to the second column without the first column. Also, remember that the rate of growth was constant throughout. So why is the second column so outrageous and the first so believable? This example shows why a simple compound interest problem can be so perplexing. What geometric progression teaches us is the importance of starting and the importance of building a sustainable growth over a long period of time.

Hole 1	$ 0.10	Hole 10	$ 51.20
Hole 2	$ 0.20	Hole 11	$ 102.40
Hole 3	$ 0.40	Hole 12	$ 204.80
Hole 4	$ 0.80	Hole 13	$ 409.60
Hole 5	$ 1.60	Hole 14	$ 819.20
Hole 6	$ 3.20	Hole 15	$ 1,638.40
Hole 7	$ 6.40	Hole 16	$ 3,276.80
Hole 8	$12.80	Hole 17	$ 6,553.60
Hole 9	$25.60	Hole 18	$13,107.20

This next example of geometric progression is one I created years ago to demonstrate the power of compounding by a simple contrasting example. There are two options presented both earning 10.0% a year. In Option 1 you fund a $3,000 IRA contribution for only the first 8 years you start working, then you stop making contributions but let it grow until year 40. In Option 2 you make no IRA contributions during the first 8 years you start working. Then starting in year 9 through year 40 you make 32 contributions of $3,000 each. Which strategy do you think produces a better result in the end, saving $24,000 or saving $96,000?

The Effects of 10.0% Compound Interest

Year	Option 1 Contribution	Option 1 Balance	Option 2 Contribution	Option 2 Balance
1	$ 3,000	$ 3,300		
2	3,000	6,930		
3	3,000	10,923		
4	3,000	15,315		
5	3,000	20,147		
6	3,000	25,462		
7	3,000	31,308		
8	3,000	37,738		
9		41,512	$3,000	$ 3,300
10		45,664	3,000	6,930
11		50,230	3,000	10,923
12		55,253	3,000	15,315
13		60,778	3,000	20,147
14		66,856	3,000	25,462
15		73,542	3,000	31,308
16		80,896	3,000	37,738
17		88,985	3,000	44,812
18		97,884	3,000	52,594
19		107,672	3,000	61,153
20		118,439	3,000	70,568
21		130,283	3,000	80,925
22		143,312	3,000	92,317
23		157,643	3,000	104,849
24		173,407	3,000	118,634
25		190,748	3,000	133,798
26		209,823	3,000	150,477
27		230,805	3,000	168,825
28		253,885	3,000	189,007
29		279,274	3,000	211,208
30		307,201	3,000	235,629
31		337,921	3,000	262,492
32		371,713	3,000	292,041
33		408,885	3,000	324,545
34		449,773	3,000	360,300
35		494,751	3,000	399,630
36		544,226	3,000	442,893
37		598,648	3,000	490,482
38		658,513	3,000	542,830
39		724,364	3,000	600,413
40		796,801	3,000	663,755
Total	**$ 24,000**	**$796,801**	**$96,000**	**$663,755**

The results from compounding $24,000 in savings over a 40-year period ($3,000 per year for only the first 8 years) versus compounding $96,000 in savings over a 32-year period ($3,000 per year beginning in year 9 and extending to year 40) are dramatic. It is hard to believe that saving $24,000 over the first eight years produces a greater ending account balance than saving $96,000 from year nine through year 40. Yet it is true!

This chart demonstrates that with a constant rate of savings one-half of the money you will have 40 years from now will come from your first 8 years of savings! This is the proof that starting to save as soon as you begin working is perhaps the most reliable way to become financially independent.

I've have been asked how this chart will differ if you increase your rate of savings with inflation over time. After 40 years of saving that grows with inflation each year, one-half of the final balance comes from your first 11 years of savings.

With personal savings, your pay increases at or hopefully above the inflation rate. Even under this scenario, half the money you will have amassed 40 years from now in your savings and investment accounts will be from the capital you saved in the earliest years.

Buried within this simple chart is all the conviction one needs as to why someone would want to start saving as soon as one starts to have an income. This chart is something I want to encourage you to share with your children, grandchildren and other young people you care about. This information can certainly empower their future if they put geometric progression to work for themselves. What better use of our knowledge of this concept than to spread the news and help others as well as ourselves. A Point to Remember - Start saving as soon as you start working, it really matters: One-half of the money you will have in your IRA 40 years after you started saving will come from your first several years of savings!

Geometric Progression

Geometric progression teaches us that the power of compounding can produce staggering results.

The Wealth Equation:

Wealth = (Contribution + Beginning Balance) x Rate of Return x Time

Contribution

You add this amount each year to your investment accounts.

Rate of Return

The higher the average earnings rate the greater the ending wealth. Earning high rates of return requires patience, prudence and knowledge skillfully applied. I will teach you how to do that in this book.

Hyper growth rates (100% and more a year) in a business you own, or hold stock or stock options in, are typically only sustainable for a few years. This opportunity is most often found in the very early phase of a new or developing industry.

High sustained rates of growth (30% to 70% a year) in a business you own is possible for a limited period. A string of five or so of these years can produce a very powerful economic result.

Good above-average growth rates (15% to 30% a year) in a business are possible on a 15 to 20 year basis, with a good business market and within a growing industry.

Hyper growth rates in real estate are rare. Most of the time hyper growth occurs because of rezoning or subdivision of land. High sustained rates of return with real estate are also very rare but can occur in special growth circumstances.

Good above-average rates of return in real estate are easiest to accomplish in a strong economic marketplace. This is one of the reasons why you hear that "location, location, location" is so important in real estate investing. Location also refers to being in a strong underlying business environment.

Hyper growth rates in stocks are inevitably followed by a precipitous decline. These are dangerous cycles for the long-term investor. If you happen to benefit from one, you should realize that the faster the gains the more likely the fall. The more the gains are based on speculation rather than current profits the more likely this is a bubble. The dot com boom was just such an event.

High sustained returns from stocks investments occur during periods of strong economic growth where profits are able to grow over a sustained period. The use of emerging-market labor to produce goods at low costs (higher profit) was just such an event. They can also occur by taking on greater risk (small value stocks) and holding these risky assets over a long period.

Good above-average rates of return from stocks can be found in strong economic times propelled by regular advances in general productivity and profitability.

Time
The longer the time you let an investment compound, generally the greater the results. People who invest over 40 years usually produce much greater wealth than people who invest over 20 years, for example.

Time is the most controllable of the factors that determines wealth. Someone who starts saving or investing in their late 20s has a much easier time arriving at financial independence than someone who waits to begin saving or investing until they are in their 40s.

Grandparent Geometric Progression
If at birth, each grandparent gave $5,000 to his or her grandchild, the grandchild would start with an account of $20,000. The following table shows how that investment would grow over time at 10% and at 15%. It also takes the 15% result

and restates that back into *today's* dollars, assuming a 4% inflation rate. Taxes were not taken into consideration.

It is surprising how much money can be generated from a single $20,000 investment. It is also impressive to note how much more money is generated by a 15% return versus a 10% return.

Geometric Progression - Single Contribution

Age	10% Growth	15% Growth	15% Inf. Adjusted
0	$ 20,000	$ 20,000	$20,000
20	134,550	327,331	149,389
35	562,049	2,663,510	674,975
50	2,347,817	21,673,149	3,049,685
65	9,807,415	176,355,748	13,779,154

If you look at the ending numbers for the non-inflation, adjusted growth, these totals seem unbelievable. I call future money "Funny Money", as it is very difficult to understand. When you inflation adjust long-term nominal numbers (Funny Money) then you are better able to understand these numbers. I find growing a onetime $20,000 contribution to thirteen million present value dollars to be substantial. Could you retire at 65 on 13 million in today's dollars that your grandparents left you as a gift at birth? This is an outstanding example of how time creates a powerful geometric progression.

One instrument that can utilize long time-periods is a Dynasty Trust. Most states allow a 99 year life and some permit an indefinite life for Dynasty Trusts today.

Rule of 72
There is a simple rule called the rule of 72 which determines how quickly your money will double. Take the number 72 and divide it by the annual rate of return and you get how many years it will take to double your investment.

If you earn 7.2% on an after-tax basis, it would take 10 years for your money to double in value. If you are not taxed and you earn a 14.4% total return, on average, each year, your initial investment would double, on average, every 5 years.

Add a Zero
This is a fun investment concept. It works like this. You buy something for say a $100 and then sell it for $1,000 dollars. This is doubling your money 3.3 times. A very profitable trick when you can pull it off.

This is almost always comes from exploiting a market inefficiency. Examples of doing this can be found in real estate where growth comes to an area you bought in some years ago. Rezoning that property can create a lot of gain in a short amount of time. It also happens with collectibles. You stumble on to an unknowledgeable seller, say an estate, and buy an item for $100 that you know you can sell today for $1,000.

Occasionally it is possible to add two zeros. Make no mistake this is very rare, but most profitable. This is doubling your money 6.6 times! Say you buy a property for $100,000 and are able to subdivide it 20 years later after the area develops and sell off the new parcels for a total of $10,000,000.

Just asking the question of how long will this investment take to add a zero starts to change your thinking and makes you look for this kind of opportunity.

Make no mistake this is speculative investing and you should limit the portion of your overall portfolio that you invest in this way.

How Bonds Create a Geometric Progression
Bonds create the simplest form of geometric progression. The interest income from bonds increases your initial investment. However, most bonds are subject to income taxation at ordinary income tax rates, thus reducing the rate at which the initial investment compounds each year.

How Stocks Create a Geometric Progression
Stocks have two earning components. First, stocks have dividends of 0-3% of market value, and dividends are taxable

now at a reduced rate of 15%, instead of the ordinary income tax rate of 38.5%. Second, stocks have market appreciation. The total return (dividend and price appreciation), for stocks averages 7% more than the underlying inflation rate. At 7%, you double your purchasing power about every 10 years. When inflation averages around 3.0%, your money doubles its nominal value (real purchasing power) every 7.2 years.

Stocks have on average only a 1% dividend rate (Source: Morningstar 12-31-2002). Most people who use just stocks and bonds for their investment portfolios must use up a portion of their principal every year in retirement. What most people need are regular monthly distributions from their stocks or stock mutual fund accounts. Most stocks and mutual funds give you the option for automatic reinvestment of dividends or the choice to have these paid out. During retirement, you can keep a reasonable cash buffer to minimize the amount of transactions necessary to meet your monthly withdrawal needs.

How Real Estate Creates a Geometric Progression
Real estate has three investment components making it the most complex in calculating total return. The first component is net after tax cash flow. This is rent, less cash expenses and income taxes. Included in the cash expenses is the loan payment. The loan is made up of both interest and principal. When the loan on real estate is new, interest expense is high and the principal pay down on the loan is low. The second component is the required new capital contribution each month. This is the principal payment portion of the loan payment. This component changes your investment and, in turn, your yield. Investment return in real estate is often stated on an Internal Rate of Return (IRR) basis to account for the ongoing capital investment when paying down a loan. The third component is the market appreciation of the underlying asset.

Real estate is one of the best assets to hold in retirement because it has a high income component that keeps up with inflation over time. The underlying asset also appreciates. Once you have history with your real estate it is easier to sleep at night knowing your income will continue to keep up with, or ahead of, inflation for the long term and that the underlying asset will also grow with, or ahead of, inflation.

The mind once expanded to the dimensions of larger ideas, never returns to its original size.

- Oliver Wendell Holmes

Chapter 2 - Income Sources

Income to save or to live on comes from one of the following sources. Each income source has unique characteristics. The skills necessary to invest wisely with each income source are easily identified and can be learned.

Employees:
    Employee
    Self Employed

Business Owners:
    Active Business Owner
    Passive Business Owner

Passive Assets

Inheritance / Sudden Wealth / Sportsperson / Entertainer

All Income Earners
Nearly all investors will experience some significant investment mistakes. The most common mistake is made with liquid investments like stocks. When an investor believes that it is possible to time markets they feel the need to make this work for them. Missing out on the early large gains in a hot market is a seductive beacon for late participation. The magazines and television shows like to promote the big gain stories. These stories sound promising but they will cost you dearly sooner or later if you use them as an investment guide. Chase enough hot sectors and you will experience more big falls than rapid gains.

Employees

Employees work for an employer. Employees are paid weekly or bimonthly by paycheck. This income is subject to regular income taxes and payroll taxes. Employees are given a benefits package that often includes medical insurance, and dental insurance and occasionally some other benefits as well. Retirement plan contributions are typical with midsize and larger companies. Sometimes these are matching contributions to a 401(k) plan and at other times they are direct company contributions to a qualified plan that you invest in over time. Some employees also receive stock options, which are a form of ownership.

Employees typically are savers and invest in stocks, bonds and, once in a while, in collectibles. Their real estate participation is usually limited to a primary home, sometimes a second home, occasionally residential rental property and some real estate mutual funds called REIT's.

The preferred saving vehicle of an employee today is often a 401(k) plan at their place of employment. It is one of the best ways to "Pay Yourself First". When your company plan provides an employer match, this program is even more powerful. Increase your participation up to the maximum level allowed as soon as you can, typically 15% of your gross annual pay.

Stock options may be an opportunity you have. These can be a valuable way to build wealth. There are times when stock options granted are not worth exercising. But this does not mean that this form of compensation is not valid. If your organization does well, stock options can provide a real boost to your quest for financial independence. What should you do with the money you get from exercising a stock option? This is money you are getting for building a business. We believe it should be reinvested not consumed. Or at least the largest portion of these funds should be reinvested after paying your taxes. The exception to this would be for using it for the down payment on a home.

When you leave a company you have the option to cash out your 401(k) plan or to roll it over into an IRA. This is long term money and you should roll it over 99.9% of the time.

The financial skills needed by most employees are a savings habit of "Paying Yourself First" combined with the knowledge and behavior to be a successful long-term investor. I will teach you how to do both of these in this book.

Self Employed
Historically this group has been made up of physicians, dentists, attorneys, accountants, architects, computer consultants, independent financial planners, construction and maintenance professionals. The ranks of independent contractors have grown steadily and today this can include almost any profession. The college educational system in America today does not provide adequate business training for the self employed. Especially lacking are sales and marketing training and financial management skills. All this can be obtained from the after market.

Making more money is not the magic cure-all this group thinks it is for financial peace of mind. When they make more money, they typically adjust their consumption spending up to a higher level, and within a short time they are back in financial stress.

Financial independence is created when you have passive income from investments sufficient to cover your living expenses and keep up with inflation over time.

The key for the Self Employed is to learn to "Pay Yourself First". This group can build their self employed business into a business asset that can be sold. The value can vary from the salvage value of their equipment plus their accounts receivable, to two times last year's owner's profit, plus accounts receivable.

A few self employed individuals have a building to sell at the end of their career. I have run the numbers and find that if you plan on staying in a location for seven or more years, you are typically better off buying your facility. In larger buildings of course this is often not practical. However, in office condominiums or stand-alone buildings, it is most desirable.

Active Business Owners

Here you are the business owner, or one of several owners. You have learned to build and use systems to create consistency and assure quality. The company is not dependent on you for its continuation. The systems and their continual evolution is the cornerstone of an Active Business operation.

An Active Business owner often has a number of well-developed skill sets. They are skilled with financial reports, improving the bottom line, setting high standards (leadership) managing people (accountability), dealing with people problems, marketing, selling, public speaking, negotiating, delegating, meeting deadlines, organizing tasks, listening to customers, risk management, monitoring the marketplace, and banking. It takes most people 15 to 20 years to learn this full complement of skills.

If all of this sounds like a lot to take on, or just takes too much time and effort, then perhaps this is not your calling. An Active Business owner must be able to deal with failure and not lose sight of the original goal. Failure and setbacks are part of the business process, a part that must be managed so as not to be fatal to the organization. Failures are your best teachers. Early recognition of mistakes that result in cash flow loss is essential to staying solvent over time.

Some of you may be wondering why anyone would want to put themselves through all of this. Well, some people love it.

A universal principal of life is:

All Life Seeks More Life for Itself and its Community.

When you are a good leader and you have developed a successful organization helping lots of people, you and your employees get tremendous satisfaction from the difference you are making. Being the center of positive forward momentum is a powerfully fulfilling experience.

An Active Business Owner has a business that can be sold in the market place for a value several times that of a Self Employed business. First, the business is typically larger because of role delegation. Second, the business is more stable after a sale, thus it commands a higher multiple on owner's profit in a sale.

For most Active Business owners this will be their largest asset. When an Active Business owner sells his (her) business, his success is now based on passive rather than active assets. If the owner has been a good saver in the past and has learned the lessons of passive income creation then he typically does a good job with his proceeds. If he lacks sufficient saving and passive investing experience then he is likely to make some serious and costly mistakes in learning this new skill. The wise business owner will surround himself with good advisors to shorten the learning time and cost. Direct real estate investing is often a good passive investment activity for this type of person.

It is easy to think when you receive a large sum for your business that you are a financial wizard. Obviously, you were a smart Active Business owner in your particular industry, but that does *not* mean you are a talented passive investment manager.

Many Active Investors (Business Owners) are often weak savers. The process of Active Investing is more like spending than it is like saving. With Active Investing (Equity Building), the most important thing is building the business. Unless the owner has experienced saving they will need to develop their spending discipline.

One of the most interesting things I observed from my clients while at MGA was that no matter how much money they made, this did not guarantee them a good savings habit. This was true with both Active Investors (Business Owners) and Self Employed Business Owners (doctors, dentists, CPA's, attorneys).

Savings skills create a discipline in your personal spending. Investing skills create sustainable purchasing power from passive assets and increased wealth over time.

Passive Business Owner

There are two basic forms of being a Passive Business Owner. The first would be a business with a limited involvement after a short initial start-up. Real estate ownership would be one example. The second would be an evolution of an Active Business Owner into the Chairman of the Board. Your involvement is on a review basis rather than in the daily management.

Real Estate is considered passive because the level of personal daily involvement is much less than found in an Active Business. It is also possible to find professional management for your real estate that will do a good job managing the income flow from this asset. As with any other asset you own, it is still a good idea to be involved in the key decisions of the managers, as no one cares as much about the success of your assets as you do. The rules for success in real estate investing and ongoing management are simpler than with stock investing.

A Passive Business is one with strong business work flow and with personnel and financial systems in place. In order to move from an Active to a Passive Business the owner(s) must learn to replace themselves in the business. They must first become good at delegating and then evolve systems for the work they previously performed. The more powerful, dedicated and charismatic the business owner, the more people it is likely to take to replace his or her responsibilities. If you keep having trouble finding a replacement then perhaps you are asking too much from a single person.

There is a unique quality found in someone with ownership: they care. Caring combined with wisdom, confidence, action and a resolute positive belief creates excellence and manifestation.

The best way to stimulate someone to adopt a high level of caring is to provide them with the ownership reward. If given too easily, however, it loses its value.

A Passive Business ownership typically has an enterprise value that can be sold. A Passive Business typically sells for a greater multiple of the owner's profit than an Active Business. The sale price can be six to twelve times the profit of the business after normalizing profits for things like excess compensation to the owner. The sale of a mature business can provide a substantial boost in reaching financial independence.

Passive Assets
These are income producing, or growth in value, assets (not a business) that do not require management of the underlying activity. This includes financial assets such as stocks, futures, commodities, bonds, loans, and investment grade collectibles.

Success at managing these assets requires knowledge, discipline and perseverance. The most effective way to become successful is to first obtain a base of knowledge about these assets yourself, through reading and or instruction. Personal experience is the next step. Using a financial advisor can be helpful. The selection of your financial advisor is most important. The values and strategies used by an advisor are critical in your development. We will cover this in more detail later.

Inheritance / Sudden Wealth / Sportsperson / Entertainer
This income typically comes from an inheritance (yours or your spouse's), an insurance award, or from a profession like that of a sportsman or actor/actress. There are many challenges to receiving sudden wealth. We will touch just briefly on the subject here. We have another book under development called *Families and Money The Entitlement Trap™* that deals exclusively with this subject. You can visit our website http:// healthywealth.com for more information.

The earlier in life you expect a substantial inheritance the greater the negative effect this windfall can have on your self-reliance and your subsequent success with money.

The Entitlement Trap™ is a dynamic process between the provider and the receiver. Financial support to a child or grandchild is given to help them get ahead in life. Unfortunately, most of the time a gift simply artificially raises their standard of living. A gift that raises one's standard of living beyond what one's income (or assets) creates results in a dependency. This is because the receiver either expects that same gift the following year or month, or needs this gift each year or month to maintain their standard of living. Dependency in an adult robs them of their self-worth. It slowly erodes their self-motivation and determination for self-reliance.

What most gift givers desire is to give a gift that enables the child to have a better life. It has not been my experience that parents or grandparents want to deliberately undermine the self-reliance and self-worth of their children or grandchildren.

It is often the case that a dependency relationship is created between the one continuing to provide financial assistance and the one receiving it. Even in college, the dynamics of dependency around family money can be well entrenched. Neither the giver nor the receiver really intended to create a dependency that trapped the receiver and robbed them of their self-esteem and drive for self-sufficiency.

It has been my experience that what both the giver and the receiver most want is an empowered life. This requires structuring gifts in a way to avoid creating dependency and facilitate creating self-reliance. The responsibility for this is with the giver. It is possible, but more difficult, for the receiver to create this discipline.

There are a variety of solutions we have developed to have gifts create self-sufficiency rather than dependency. One way is to create an exchange in gift giving. The exchange is important in maintaining self worth and breaking dependency, as the gift is now earned.

For example, when providing college education support, I recommend establishing written rules that require a certain performance and participation by the receiver. Failure to comply must be met with the promised enforcement. This performance requirement with a real consequence is enough to create an exchange. When they get out on their own this is what life demands, and it is better to learn these lessons early at home.

Inheriting substantial amounts of money can be an emotionally troubling responsibility for the beneficiary. If the beneficiary has grown up receiving regular life-style financial assistance you should not be surprised when they do not handle their inheritance very responsibly. After all, they were trained to be financially irresponsible.

The key to success and improved self worth regarding inheritance is in preparing the beneficiary to be self-reliant before they ever have access to these funds. It is also important to learn to be a good passive investor. Financial planners can help. Finding and learning to work with a good real estate advisor, accountant, and attorney are also important. There is no substitute, however, for each child learning to become self-reliant, and most important learn to save.

When an inheritance is used to produce a lifetime of income, rather than consumed for a better life-style today it raises self esteem. Many things can be done in a will to encourage this outcome. Care has to be taken to avoid creating too much control, which can actually result in the opposite outcome than was intended.

Sudden wealth coming from one's profession can also be a very challenging situation. The key issue is: will enough of this money be used to create a lifetime of income or will it be consumed in short-term life-style needs today?

If used primarily to raise present-day life-style, a precipitous fall in that life-style will result once the high earning years end. This will require the sale of assets, and a substantial reduction in spending. This adjustment can be a real blow to one's self-worth.

The solution here is to take a substantial portion of the funds earned in the peak years and deploy them into investment assets that will provide a lifetime of income. High risk high reward investments are not appropriate when the top earning years could be limited. We recommend that 20% to 50% of annual income be placed into investments designed to provide a lifetime of income and a current income-tax shelter. Commercial real estate offers an attractive investment solution for the primary portion of the investment allocation for these high income earners.

Chapter 3 - Saving, Equity Building and Investing

Saving, equity building and investing are all done to build an economic battery. Once developed this economic battery generates income and has stored value that can be exchanged. This is often the purpose of saving for financial independence. It is what trusts do to pass along wealth and have it serve the mission of the family or financially empower family members. It is useful to make a distinction between saving, equity building and investing.

Savings can only happen when you spend less than you make after taxes. Savings is putting money into an account where it will be invested. Learning to save is the primary underpinning to dealing with money successfully. This is typically done from your paycheck and a bonus. A business may also save money each month and pay it out as a bonus, or keep it as a reserve. More people create financial independence through savings than any other method. Not everyone can discipline themselves to be good savers. Everyone should learn to save, as it improves your financial discipline.

Equity building is the second way to build your economic battery and create financial independence. This is the growth in value of assets that can be used to later produce income to live off or equity that can be sold. The most common forms of equity building are investment in real estate and owning a business that can later be sold. Equity building is both a forced savings program and appreciation strategy. It is more akin to spending than it is to saving. People who find they are better at putting in their time and labor into a project or are good at finding deals are more likely to use this wealth creation strategy.

Business equity building has several components. You start with growing a business in size and then in profits. It is the profit that creates the wealth. As the business grows it needs more operating cash and reserves. This is business savings. Banks recognize the need for this and will request you build up your capital reserves as you grow. Some businesses need more reserves than others. Most businesses should build up a cash flow reserve equal to 3-12 months of fixed operating expenses once they are out of survival. Building value in a business requires investing back in the business so it remains competitive and can evolve. A business should also develop systems to evolve efficiency and productivity. In a professional business this looks a little different. Here you would build systems that model the best practices and allow the staff to do as much of the work as possible. The better the systems the more valuable the business.

Real estate equity building has three primary components. The first is the systematic pay down of the loan from the purchase and any subsequent improvements. This is in reality a forced savings program. Equity or stored economic value is created this way. The second is growth in the underlying value of the land and building. The third form of real estate equity building comes from adding value to a property by doing improvements.

Investing is how you apply funds that you have saved. It is the purchase of stocks, bonds, real estate, a business or collectibles.

Savings
The best way to save is to "Pay Yourself First". "Paying Yourself First" is when you treat savings as a required activity – like paying on your mortgage or paying your electric bill. You would never consider not paying your loan payment or a utility bill. "Paying Yourself First" is a way of adhering to the

requirement to save each month, in the same way you adhere to making a loan payment or paying a utility bill. "Paying Yourself First" is about learning to make your monthly saving account additions mandatory, not discretionary.

The Three Savings Accounts
6-Month Reserve

You need a reserve account to cover six months of your required average monthly cash outflows, exclusive of taxes and new savings. This account should be invested in a short term bond fund or held in a money market fund. Over time, as your monthly outflows increase, you need to increase this reserve account. This is your most important account and it should be built first. Once you have three months of savings built-up you can then split your total monthly savings between this account and an IRA or 401(k) account.

Financial Assets Accounts

There are two primary types of financial asset accounts: retirement accounts and personal investment accounts.

Personal investment accounts are typically held in your name at a brokerage firm or with a mutual fund. The new contributions that go into a personal investment account are made with after-tax dollars, and the income they earn each year is subject to taxation.

Retirement accounts include IRA's, 401(k) plans, and other employer qualified plans. Retirement accounts are typically funded with deductible (pre-tax) dollars, except for Roth IRA accounts. Income generated in a retirement account is not taxed. Distributions of both principal and income from a retirement account are fully taxable as ordinary income when received, except with a Roth IRA.

With Roth IRAs, your initial contributions are not deductible, hence both the principal and the deferred income are not taxable when distributed.

Passive Income Account

This is a holding account used to purchase real estate or to make an investment in a business from which you will be able to derive passive investment income (for example, a franchise business where you have a manager running the business for you).

Investing

This is what you do with the funds added to your savings accounts. It includes buying financial assets like stocks and bonds, real estate, a business, paying off debt in an accelerated manner, or parking the funds in a money market account. Investing is when you buy things that will provide a future income stream or future appreciation that will be converted to an income stream. Buying a house, for example, is not an investment *per se*. It will not provide you with a future income stream, unless you are planning to trade down at retirement, in which case the trade down portion is an investment.

We will cover the activity of investing in depth in the investment section.

Active Business ownership is the most unusual of the investment assets. Both employee types (employee, self employed) and both business types (active business owner, and passive business owner) can have an investment in the business they work in. Employees can own stock or stock options of their employer. Self employed business owners may be able to sell their business at some point. Active and passive business ownership typically has a sale value.

The Power of Saving

While at MGA I did a study of our 4,000+ clients. I sought to identify what the common characteristics were of our top 20% of clients in terms of income, wealth and financial peace of mind. I also examined the contrasting characteristics of our most financially challenged clients. I found that the key to being successful with money (creating it, growing it and achieving financial independence because of it) was the savings habit.

This is big news. If you want to empower someone to be good with money then the skill they must have is to learn to save. If you teach them to become an accomplished saver then the more money they make, the better off they will become in terms of income, wealth, and financial peace of mind. If you are planning on leaving money to your children or grandchildren through a trust, it is most important that you teach them how to become good savers before you leave them the money.

This understanding is an example of how to use a technology I developed called "Start With the Answer™. Now that you know what makes a person better with money, you can focus your efforts to that end. Without this insight, the task of training your children about money, investing, and the financial world seems overwhelming.

Developing a Saving Habit
Anyone who saves can retire or enjoy financial independence. The earlier you start saving and investing, the easier it will be to retire or achieve lifetime financial independence. The higher the percentage of your income you spend today, the longer it will take to retire or reach lifetime financial independence.

How Much Should You Save?
A reasonable rate of savings for most people is 10% to 20% of their gross earnings. When you are first developing the savings habit, target to get to 10%, and never go below this level once you get there. A savings level of 15% is a solid level and is enough for most people. A savings rate of 20% or more is a Power Saver.

People who have a short period of high income should save 20% to 50% of their gross income in the high earning years.

The 24 & 36-Month Rule
A remarkable thing about saving and building any new habit is that once you repeat it at least 21 consecutive times, you have broken through and made that action a part of your present beliefs. I observed that nearly all clients embarking on a new savings discipline are reliable for the first few months, but after that the real test begins. If they make it 12 straight months,

things look promising. Make it 24 months and they have created a discipline. After 36 months, the discipline is as solid as month old cement, and a healthy set of beliefs have formed to support the saving practice.

What can we learn from people that struggle in creating this habit? First, it is far more important to build the savings habit than to save the right amount. As long as you are saving at your target level EVERY month, you are building the savings muscle, experiencing in your body what it is to save money every month, and creating reinforcing beliefs about saving money.

It is much better to start with a lower target savings rate and succeed at saving than it is to get to the optimum level as soon as you start saving. For most people a 10% savings level is the right target level. For first time savers a 5% savings rate may be a better initial target.

Everyone should get to at least a 10% savings rate, not everyone should start with a 10% savings rate. Remember building the savings habit (experience) is much more valuable than winning the self imposed savings competition.

Some people (entrepreneurs) are better at investing than saving. If this is your situation then do both. Reduce your target savings rate (never eliminate it), then fire away at your investment opportunities. Remember savings is your economic battery to start business investment opportunities. Real estate direct ownership is a good choice for entrepreneurs learning to be passive investors.

Equity Building

Real Estate
What is your home ownership?
A.   Your largest investment?
B.   The key to creating wealth?
C.   Your primary asset for financial independence?
D.   Your best income tax deduction?
E.   What your kids will get when you are gone?

F. Your most expensive life-style outlay?

G. What drives your life-style costs?

Many people are confused about this issue and for good reason. If you plan to trade down your home for a less costly home some day then the part that you trade down is in fact an investment. If you do not substantially trade down the value of your home someday then your home is a life-style choice and a substantial part of your estate when you die. Your home should for the most part not be seen as an investment, as it produces no income. It is a life-style choice you are paying for yesterday, today and tomorrow. Your equity in this asset belongs to your estate and upon your death can be converted to an income producing asset for your children.

When you own real estate for investment purposes you are equity building. Often you can exchange your time and energy for adding value to your investment. This is common in simple cleanup and fix up activities like landscaping, painting and remodeling. Paying down principal is equity building if you maintain your payment level. Lowering your interest rate is equity building. Improving the property is equity building. Converting the property to a higher use such as in a commercial property from industrial use to industrial and office is equity building. Improving the aesthetics and or function of the property is equity building. Increasing the cash flow is equity building when it is beyond normal inflation of rents.

Chapter 4 - Investment Fundamentals

The charts, graphs, tables and examples contained in this book are offered for purposes of illustration only. They do not imply the return that may be available on any particular investment.

Introduction to Investing
The science of investment management is only about 100 years old, and is still a developing field. The past twenty-five years have seen an enormous increase in the amount, quality, and availability of research data. The fundamental precepts of investment management are being established today. Old beliefs, such as, "employing market timing to avoid big losses" are giving way to newer truths, such as it takes more than ten years for returns to approach their expected levels.

Investment Asset Classes
The following outline summarizes the major classes of assets for consideration in an investment portfolio. Each investor, either by default or from careful consideration, builds a portfolio from these asset classes.

Fixed Income (Domestic / International / Emerging Market)
Money Market
Short Term
Intermediate
Long Term

Equities (Domestic / International / Emerging Markets)
  Large Capitalization (Full Index)
  Large Capitalization High Book-to-Market (Value)
  Large Capitalization Low Book-to-Market (Growth)
  Large Capitalization - Sectors
  Small Capitalization (Full Index)
  Small Capitalization High Book-to-Market (Value)
  Small Capitalization Low Book-to-Market (Growth)
  Small Capitalization Sectors
Real Estate
  Residential - Single Family / Apartment
  Commercial
  Land
Commodities
Collectibles

U.S. Asset Class Performance

Roger Ibbotson and Rex Sinquefield, graduates of the University of Chicago, conducted a landmark study on the performance of the major classes of financial assets since 1926. Their work provides an excellent basis for understanding the relative performance and volatility of different classes of assets.

Returns / Volatility 1926-2003

Asset Class	Compound Annual Return %	Average Annual Return %	Volatility % (1 Standard Deviation)
Inflation	3.0	3.1	4.3
30 Day Treasury Bills	3.7	3.8	3.2
Large Stocks	10.2	12.0	20.1
Small Stocks	11.8	16.1	31.4

Source: Dimensional Fund Advisors

From this study, we learn:
- Large U.S. stocks outperformed inflation by 7.2% a year on a compound annual return basis over the last 78 years.

- Small U.S. stocks outperformed large stocks by 1.6% per year on a compound annual return basis over the last 78 years. This increased performance has come at a cost of 50% greater volatility of return (31% standard deviation versus 20% for large stocks).
- One Month T-Bills returned only 0.7% a year more on a compound basis than inflation over the last 78 years.

Stocks, Bonds, T-Bills & Inflation (1926-2003)
The Ibbotson-Sinquefield study is the basis for understanding how the major domestic classes of assets: T-Bills, Large Stocks (S&P 500) and Small Stocks have performed over long periods.

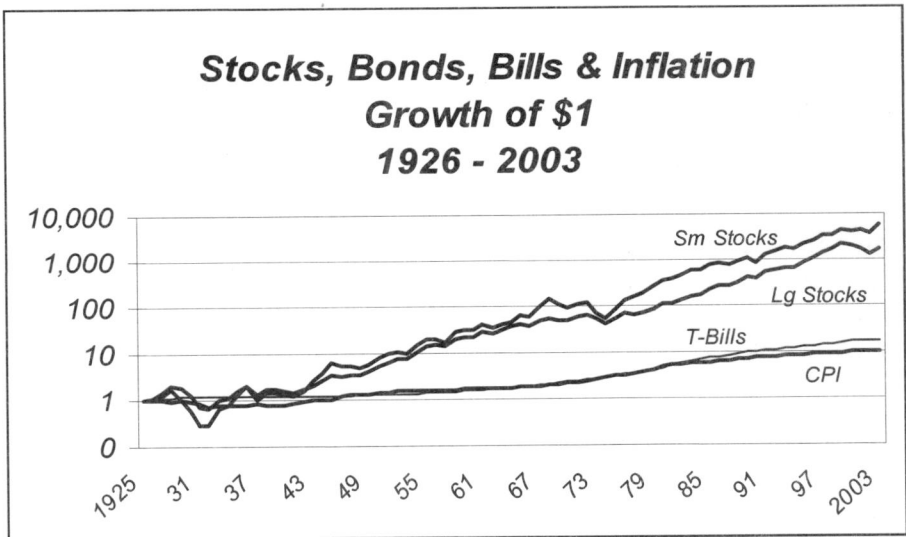

Stocks, Bonds, Bills & Inflation
Growth of $1
1926 - 2003

Source: Dimensional Fund Advisors

The previous table and graph demonstrate that in order to increase returns, you must accept higher return volatility. It also illustrates that stocks (greater return volatility) substantially outperform bonds over time.

Return Volatility – 1 Standard Deviation
Standard deviation is a statistical measure of variation from the average; just over two-thirds of all returns fall within one standard deviation of the average. Likewise, 95% of all returns

fall within two standard deviations of the average, and 99% of all returns fall within three standard deviations of the average.

Example: For the last 78 years, large stocks have had an average annual return of 12.0%, with a standard deviation of 20.1%. This means that there is a 67% probability that U.S. large stocks will have an annual return between 32.1% and -8.1%. The compound annualized return is the rate at which your money compounds. The average annual return is the mathematical average of all observed returns. One Standard Deviation = 67% probability

Maximum: 32.1% = 12.0% + 20.1%
Minimum: -8.1% = 12.0% - 20.1%

Dimensions of Return
Security Selection
Security selection is a method used by investors to identify companies that they believe will outperform other companies over some future holding period.

Example: You could hire an investment advisor, stock broker or bank trust department to choose 10 large U.S. stock companies for your portfolio. This is active security selection. This portfolio performance is compared against its appropriate benchmark. In this case, it would be a universe of all U.S. large company stocks, commonly referred to as the S&P 500.

Security selection assumes it is possible, through research, to know more than the market consensus knows about the pricing of individual stocks. It assumes it is possible to have exclusive knowledge about the market's mis-pricing of stocks at any given point in time.

Market Timing
Market timing refers to the timing of movement in and out of a particular asset class in order to either avoid losses, or participate in a stock when it is about to increase in value.

Deciding that U.S. Large Stocks will likely lose value over the next twelve months and, consequently, shifting some your large U.S. stock allocation into bonds or a money market account for the next twelve months, is an example of market timing.

Investment managers can be very seductive in their claims to have superior knowledge that will allow them to get your money out of each stock asset class before it suffers any major decline, and then return to that stock asset class in time to participate in the good periods. History strongly supports that none of these managers can actually do this over long periods of time.

Asset Allocation (Portfolio Design)
Asset allocation is the process of proportioning your investments among different asset classes.

Example: Your investment portfolio at any point in time contains a certain percentage of cash, short term bonds, medium term bonds, U.S. large stocks, U.S. small stocks, international large stocks, international small stocks, emerging market stocks, U.S. residential real estate, U.S. commercial real estate, and international real estate.

The Brinson, Hood, Singer & Beebower Studies

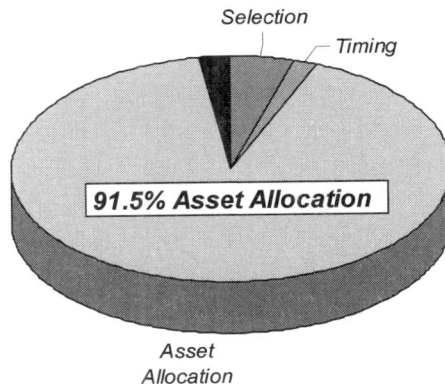

Selection
Timing
91.5% Asset Allocation
Asset Allocation

Brinson, Hood & Beebower (1983 & 1987) and Brinson, Singer & Beebower (1991) published extensive research evaluating the results of 82 pension funds in the United States to determine the influence that market timing, security selection, and portfolio design had on return. The 1983 study covered 10 years, the 1987 study covered 15 years, and the 1991 study 19 years. All three studies produced similar results.

Roger Ibbotson and Paul Kaplan performed a similar study in 1999 that looked at 10-year compound returns of 94 balanced mutual funds to determine how much of the variation in returns was explained by the asset allocation. This study concluded that on average the quarterly returns of the benchmark accounted for 90% of the variability in quarterly returns.

For investors these studies confirm how important it is to choose a portfolio design. In fact, very few financial advisors will disagree that this is the most important decision an investor will make.

The importance of these studies is very significant. They conclude, categorically, that individual investors should be far more concerned with learning how to do an effective asset allocation than with picking the right stocks, mutual funds or hot manager.

To become successful as an investor you need to fully understand the art and science of asset allocation. The investment section of this book is designed to help you improve your skills in this area.

Ask yourself if you have spent as much time learning how to design and build an investment portfolio as you spend choosing the funds or stocks in your portfolios. If your answer is no, then you are putting your efforts into the wrong area. Congratulations on purchasing and reading this book, for it is full of practical asset-allocation advice.

The above studies, and others like them, have brought to light the fact that the investment management industry, which is selling security selection and market timing, is selling you the wrong information if you want to improve your long-term performance.

The statistical proof that active security selection and active market timing lead to under performance has resulted in big changes in the way large pension managers and fiduciaries perform their investment activities.

Index funds and Exchange Traded Funds (ETF's) that offer asset class participation, with very low costs, have increased in popularity in recent years.

In the last fifteen years new investment rules have evolved that make fiduciaries (those responsible for the portfolio management of others) responsible for the burden of proof when using active security selection and market timing in their investment choices.

Because the Brinson *et al* study showed that 91.5% of the variation in return in a portfolio is determined by portfolio design, even the best stock manager will have a difficult time performing better than the index over the long haul. The 4.6% variation in return measured from security selection can be either a loss or a gain; more often, it is a variation for loss (Brinson, Singer, & Beebower, 1991).

The Vanguard Group conducted a study which determined that an active manager (one who performs non-statistical searches for undervalued companies) could potentially add a maximum of only an additional 0.5% per year in return; yet, nearly all active managers charge more than 0.5% for their services. Where does that leave you?

All investors pay a spread between the price a stock sells for and what it can be bought for. The smaller the market volume of a stock the greater the spread between the buy price and sell price. Retail investors pay a larger spread than do large mutual funds when buying the same stock or bond. Retail investors also often pay a transaction fee when purchasing or selling a stock.

The buy-sell spread can be as little as 0.125% to as much as 10% with a very small company. The spread paid for transactions under 100 shares (round lot) is larger than the spread for small lots. Lots traded in 10,000 shares by the large mutual funds get a lower spread than 100 share lots.

Commissioned advisors, brokerage houses and banks charge between 3% and 8% in up-front fees for loaded mutual funds. Results comparing loaded funds to "no-loads" show there is, in fact, no advantage to loaded funds because they usually under perform. To add insult to injury, their ongoing fees tend to be higher. According to Morningstar, the average annual administrative expense of large U.S. stock mutual funds was 1.4%, as of December 31, 2002.

Some mutual funds charge a 1.0% purchase or sell load to offset the transaction costs of the buying or selling shareholder. This load typically goes into the fund and is not paid out to a broker, financial advisor or the fund management. This kind of a load is meant to keep down turnover, and serves to protect the existing mutual fund investors from bearing the buy or sell costs of the new or exiting investors. Vanguard does this on some of its small stock funds, and it has been very successful in protecting the fund from high turnover costs. When the load increases above 1.0%, it is then reasonable to assume that this is, in fact, a sales load.

Since market timing determines only 1.7% of the variation of a portfolio's return, market-timing funds, even those with the smallest costs, have difficulty adding value over anything but a few lucky years (which is statistically expected), or when measured against the wrong benchmark.

Modern portfolio theory states that security markets are, largely, efficient. Daily prices on individual stocks reflect all historical information as well as buyers' expectations about the stock for the future. As soon as any new information is known, it is simultaneously sent electronically to thousands of analysts and is quickly reflected in pricing.

At times markets may overreact upward and downward. No reliable and repeatable method for determining and capturing these overreactions on a cost effective basis has been developed and proven.

Real Estate Returns & Volatility
Single Family Residence & Apartments

This is the safest real estate asset class to invest in because vacancy rates are typically low; however, it has the lowest income return as a percentage of the asset value. People always need housing. Vacancies tend to be a function of the net growth or decline in the job market; they usually rise in regions experiencing a sustained economic downturn. Vacancy rates for the housing market tend to be low and stable most of the time.

The income from housing tends to be 2.0% to 5.0% of market value. This is around half the income from commercial property. The low income rate reflects that the risk to the owner is low. During a recession, you are likely to have only a short vacancy in most housing markets. The exception would be in an area with a substantial shrinkage in the job market. Such an example occurred in the oil states in the early 1990s when the oil industry collapsed. Today, Texas and other oil states have diversified their economic base.

Housing price appreciation and rental appreciation are very location dependent. You get the best long-term appreciation in areas that are enjoying fast underlying growth and have a restricted supply of new local housing opportunities.

Commercial Property

Income from commercial property ranges from 6% to 12% of fair market value in most regions of the country. The current average national capitalization rate (cap rate) for commercial property is around 7.5%. This means the net income flow, before depreciation and debt service, averages 7.5% of the market value of the property. The higher the cap rate the better the income return on your investment.

Commercial property is riskier than residential property because its potential for sustained vacancies is greater. In areas that have a robust economic environment, well located properties have little trouble with vacancies, most of the time. Commercial vacancies can take many months to fill in average or slow markets. Sustained vacancies can occur during bad economic times and often require rent concessions to ultimately fill the space.

One of the ways to reduce your risk is to purchase commercial property in a region with strong, well diversified economic growth. If this can be combined with a limit on close by alternatives for new development, then you have met the two requirements for good real estate investment.

Property with a lower tenant concentration is less risky than property with a higher percentage rented to a single tenant.

The quality of the tenant is important in commercial investing. The stronger and more stable the tenant, the better the lease quality.

There are two basic types of leases: a triple net lease (NNN) and a gross lease. In a NNN lease, the tenant pays for their own utility costs, property taxes, and maintenance of most aspects of the building, except the outside walls and roof. Thus, the owner has very little expense other than the loan and the occasional new roof or exterior building maintenance. In a gross lease, the tenant usually pays only rent and their phone bill. The other utility costs, property taxes and maintenance costs are paid by the landlord. Most commercial leases are NNN today. Small square-footage leases of office space are still done as a gross lease. Short-term subleases of small spaces are also often done as a gross lease for record keeping simplicity.

Land
This is the riskiest form of real estate investment. It also has the highest potential return. Land that can be rezoned to a higher and better use, after its initial purchase, offers some of the best opportunity for gains in real estate. Often this type of investment takes decades to be fully realized. Skilled land investors with very deep pockets can shorten this time. This is not an investment asset class for the novice.

Generally, the subdivision of land tends to take many years, sometimes decades. Slow growth policies tend to hamper the pace of growth and particularly subdivision. When water supplies grow short, the pace of new development slows to a crawl. Water shortages are likely to be an even bigger problem in the future than it has been in the past. When water supplies shrink up it can take 15 to 30 years to solve the problem.

Until development can take place, raw land does not usually provide any income, unless it can be leased for farming.

Raw land can be very difficult to sell. The average selling time is often many times that of developed property. When a market is hot, land tends to sell. Conversely, when a real estate market is cold, land can be impossible to sell.

Because of the high-risk nature, and the lack of liquidity for this asset class, most investors should not hold more than 20% of their investment portfolio in raw land. Investors should not consider it as an investment until they can pay off the land and live without any income from it for at least twenty years.

Commodities

Commodities are an excellent diversifier in an asset allocation, as they tend, over time, to have the lowest correlation to stocks. Unfortunately, this asset class is hard to find in mutual fund offerings or in direct stock. Some progress is being made in offering commodities as Exchange Traded Funds (ETF's). Before long, this should solve this problem and the use of commodities in asset allocations of large pension funds and individual accounts should steadily increase.

The cost of most commodity mutual funds is also an issue and, again, the ETFs should solve this.

Collectibles

Collectibles are not for everyone; they are a unique investment, unlike any of the other asset classes. Collectibles can be your business, a hobby or an investment.

Collectibles as a hobby can be an activity that adds meaning to one's life and may or may not have a profit motive.

Collectible investing is a high risk long-term form of investing. Often the resale value of these assets can drop by 50% or more, and stay at this lower level for many years. Appreciation can be swift and dramatic in the best of times. When this type of appreciation is sustained over a number of years the best pieces can become very expensive, as has become the case with famous paintings. During a downturn, if you need the cash or lose patience with your investment, selling can be very costly.

There are a few basic ways to make money in collectibles. Really know what you are doing better than everyone else you do business with. Have a great value added process, typically in the final marketing. Get lucky over time by being in a market that becomes highly sought after.

The history of collectibles over several decades shows us that these markets have more volatility than the stock market. The downturns are often prolonged. The upturns seem to be unstoppable – until they stop, of course. The best pieces appreciate the most on both an absolute and a relative basis. Not only are these markets driven by the general economy, but they are also driven by social factors, which are often difficult to anticipate until they are realized.

There are a few very important rules to follow when investing in collectibles:
- Collect what you love. If you lose your excitement for your collection, then get rid of it while the market is still close to what you paid for it.
- Limit your investment to 4% of your net worth and 10% of your investable assets. Do not violate this rule if you are 45 or more years of age.
- Be alert that what you are doing may actually be gambling not investing. All gamblers end up paying the price – getting cleaned out. This is why the rule of limiting your investment as described above is so critical.
- You cannot time the bottom or the top of any market, and that is true for collectibles as well. The economic factors that drive the underlying demand are too complex. A successful way of dealing with rising and falling markets is to assign only three names to markets: seller's market,

buyer's market, and sideways market. Eliminate from your vocabulary such terms as the market bottom or market top. These are only identifiable after the fact, and will frustrate you if you think you should have known them in advance.

- There are three keys for collectibles to become valuable:
  - It must be desired
  - The quality should be outstanding if this is for investment
  - It must be rare
- It is much better to own a few high quality pieces than it is to own a large quantity of mediocre pieces. The best pieces will make you more money and are easier to display and store.
- Do your research. These markets are relatively inefficient and, as such, it is possible after adequate research to buy from sellers who have cash needs or who do not know the market adequately for a fraction of what it can be sold for.
- Learn from the experts in your field. One of the great things about collectibles is people love to share their passion.
- The more established the market place for a collectible, the less affordable will be the best pieces. The more established markets tend to be broader, hence, they fluctuate less than fledgling markets.
- If you want to make large profits reliably, then you first must know how much profit you are making when you buy. It also helps to sell in a better marketplace than where you are buying.

The investment principles learned here will also serve you well with other forms of investing. As you may know, it is very difficult for an individual collector to actually sell most collectibles and make a net profit, even if its retail value has gone up 50% or 100%. One of the best pieces of advice I received was to buy collectibles you loved living with, because in most cases that is all it will be good for.

Chapter 5 - Investment Strategies

The charts, graphs, tables and examples contained in this book are offered for purposes of illustration only. They do not imply the return that may be available on any particular investment.

1990 Nobel Prize for Economics
In 1990, the Nobel Prize for economics was awarded to three Americans for their achievements in investment theory. They were Harry Markowitz, William Sharpe, and Merton Miller. Their theories provide investors with practical methods for managing an investment portfolio.

Harry Markowitz
In the early 1950s, Professor Markowitz developed mathematical models of financial markets to explain the return of different portfolios. Optimized portfolios can be structured from these mathematical models.

Within the models, Professor Markowitz incorporated the expected return and volatility of each class of assets and the cross-correlation of each class of assets to all other classes of assets.

William Sharpe
Professor Sharpe's work dealt with predicting the return of an individual stock as compared to the overall market. Each stock was assigned a *beta*, or correlation coefficient to the market. The

beta compares the volatility of the returns of an individual stock with the volatility of the index. A low beta stock has less volatility than the index, and a high beta stock has more volatility than the index.

Merton Miller

Professor Merton Miller examined the factors that determine the financing choices facing a company. His theories describe the relationship between a company's capital asset structures (the strength of its balance sheet), the dividends the company would pay on its stock each quarter, and the resulting market value of that company.

How Holding Periods Affect Volatility

Holding or review periods make a real difference in the volatility of your investments.

The following four charts show an evaluation of the performance of large U.S. stocks on an annual, 5-year, 10-year, or 20-year basis during the last 78-year period, 1926-2003.

Yearly

The yearly data is quite volatile. Annual returns were positive about two-thirds of the time. Annual returns fluctuated as much as 60% from year to year and typically ranged from -10% to +30%.

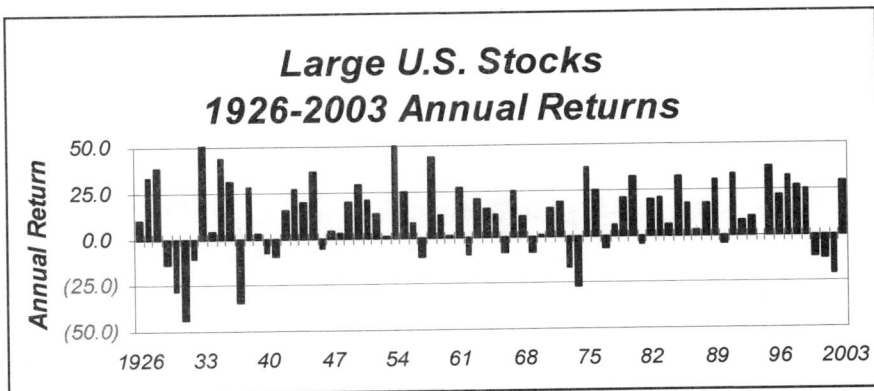

Source: Dimensional Fund Advisors

5 Years

At 5 years, the returns are still variable but mostly positive.

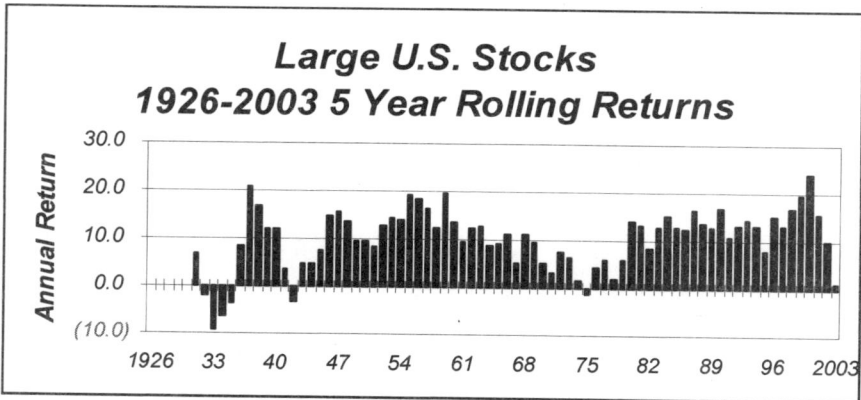

**Large U.S. Stocks
1926-2003 5 Year Rolling Returns**

(Chart: Annual Return, years 1926 to 2003)

Source: Dimensional Fund Advisors

10 Years

At 10 years, the returns become reliably positive but they still have a significant range. The fact that it takes 7 to 10 years for stock investing to return a positive return is why you will hear that unless you have at least a 10-year investment horizon you should not invest in stocks.

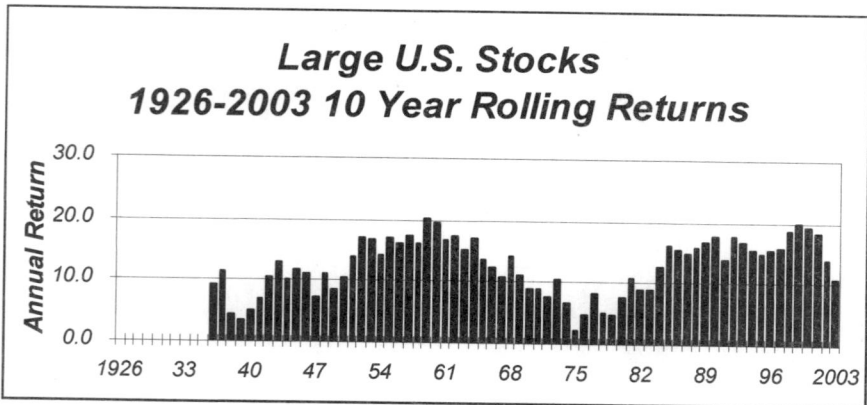

**Large U.S. Stocks
1926-2003 10 Year Rolling Returns**

(Chart: Annual Return, years 1926 to 2003)

Source: Dimensional Fund Advisors

20 Years

Evaluating your stock decision once every 20 years not only always produces a positive result but one within an acceptably narrow range. To have stocks come close to their expected return of 7% over inflation, your evaluation period should be 20 years or more.

Large U.S. Stocks
1926-2003 20 Year Rolling Returns

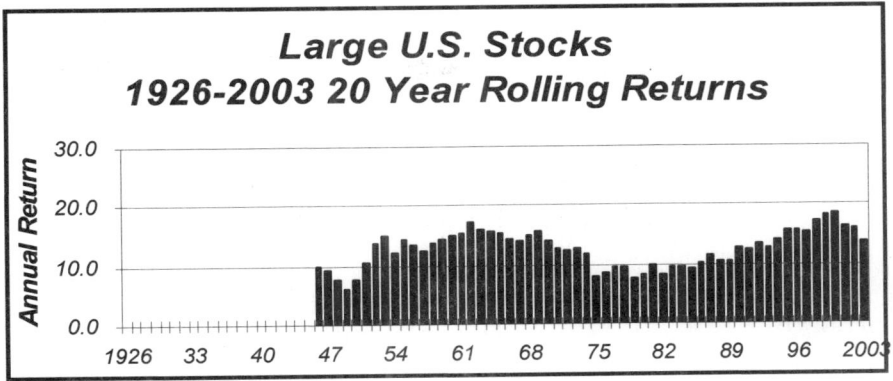

Source: Dimensional Fund Advisors

Investing's Triple Loss

Individuals sometimes experience a *triple loss* when investing because their decisions are based on emotions rather than clear thinking.

1. BUY HIGH - They buy into stocks after they have been rising for a consistent period of time.
2. SELL LOW - They sell when stocks have taken a substantial beating.
3. MISS THE RECOVERY - By doing this, they miss the recovery that follows.

Cross-Correlation / Diversification

Cross-correlation is an important mathematical concept in investing. It is the measurement of how each class of assets moves over time compared to other classes of assets.

A correlation relationship where both asset classes move in the same direction and in similar proportion to market changes is called a positive correlation. When two assets classes reflect no measurable systematic movement over time, they are deemed to have no correlation, and their correlation coefficient is measured as 0.0. When two asset classes move in opposite directions most of the time, they are said to have a negative correlation.

An ideal investment correlation relationship would be to have a perfectly negative correlation (-1.0) between two classes of assets. That means that over a period of time when one class goes down by 10%, the other asset class would go up by 10%.

Negative correlation is rare, so most of the time the best we can do is to find two asset classes that have a low positive correlation (near zero).

When we add an asset class to our portfolio that has a low correlation with the other asset classes, it reduces the overall volatility of the portfolio. The more we can combine low correlation asset classes, the lower the overall volatility of the resulting portfolio.

Many investors are aware of the need to reduce volatility by diversification. Too often, individual investors purchase different stock funds expecting this to give them diversification. However, if the underlying assets are really from the same asset class (even though all or most companies in the funds are different).

Efficient Frontier
Investment return optimization was first developed by Professor Markowitz (the 1990 Nobel Prize Laureate) in a paper published in 1953 in the *Journal of Financial Analysis.*

The efficient frontier represents the maximum return possible for each level of return volatility. It is derived by a mathematical formula that accounts for:

- The expected return of each class of assets
- The volatility of each class of assets
- The cross-correlation of each class of assets to all other classes

The problem with efficient frontier mathematical models is with the input. It is impossible to know accurately what the correct future values will be for your input variables. Garbage in is garbage out.

The expected return of each asset class is the most difficult to estimate accurately. In the short and medium-term, these vary considerably. Even after 20 years, they can still vary significantly enough to affect the outcome of this calculation. Relative return volatility and cross-correlation relationships tend to be much more stable.

Another inherent problem with optimizers is that they tend to recommend portfolios with only two asset classes. Two asset classes may be an optimal 20 year strategy but is a suboptimal 1 to 20 year strategy.

The purpose of diversification is not to maximize annual returns but to control return volatility, while maintaining a steady, high level of returns relative to what is going on in the general stock and real estate markets. One of the purposes of diversification is to help investors stay the course in the short and medium term.

The following examples show how diversification improves performance while also reducing risk. The mixes shown range from 100% of one asset class to 100% of the other asset class. What is most important to accomplish is a substantial reduction of the risk: return volatility (1 standard deviation of return variance) while gaining a little in return.

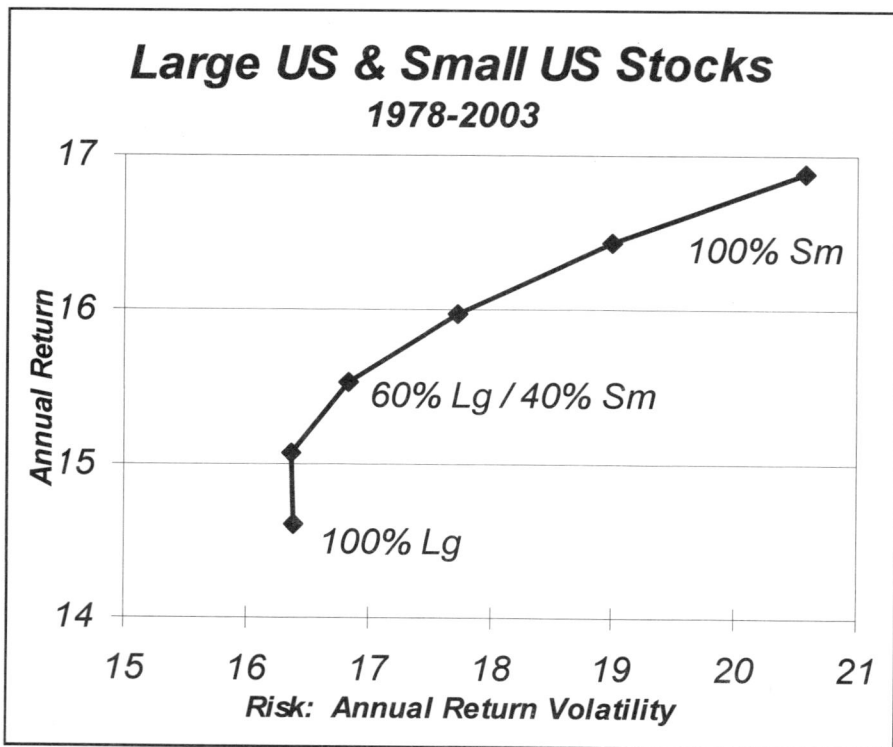

Large US & Small US Stocks
1978-2003

Source: Dimensional Fund Advisors

This chart goes from 100% large U.S. stocks to 100% small U.S. stocks. We add small U.S. stocks in 20% increments. At the point where we have added 20% small stocks we increase return by 0.5% with no change in overall return volatility. As we add more small company stock we increase return but also increase return volatility.

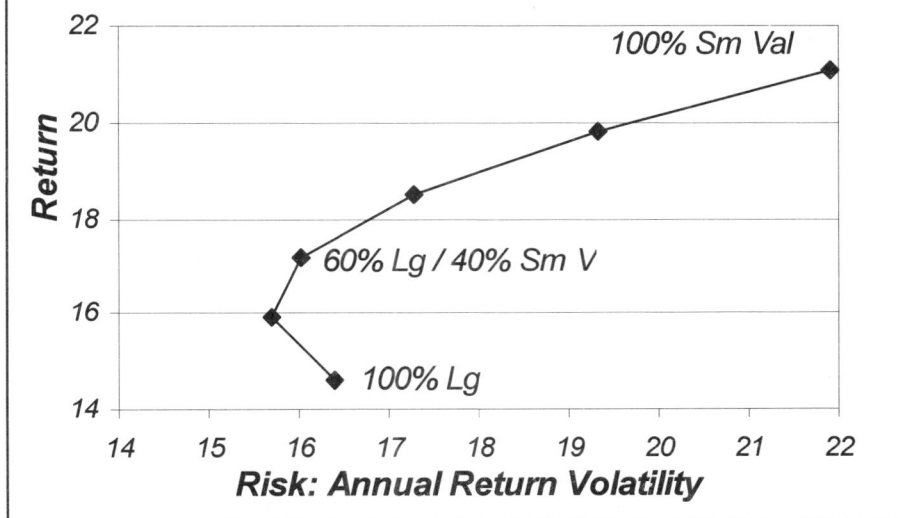

Large US & Small Value Stocks
1978 - 2003

Return

22

20

18

16

14

100% Sm Val

60% Lg / 40% Sm V

100% Lg

14   15   16   17   18   19   20   21   22

Risk: Annual Return Volatility

Source: Dimensional Fund Advisors

In this chart, we are starting with 100% large U.S. stocks and now add small U.S. value stocks in 20% increments until we end up with 100% small U.S. value stocks. We get an even better result than we did with small U.S. stocks (full index). At 60% large U.S. stocks and 40% small U.S. value stocks we still get a whopping 2.6% pickup in return and have lower return volatility. This is a significant development. U.S. small value stocks are a better diversifier than U.S. small stocks (full index).

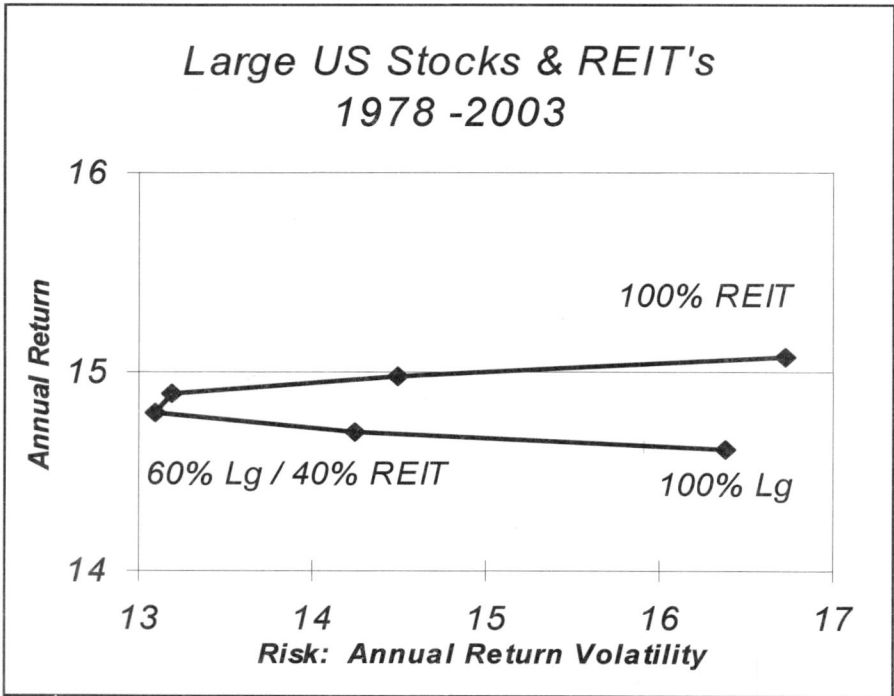

Large US Stocks & REIT's
1978 -2003

Figure: Annual Return (y-axis, 14 to 16) vs Risk: Annual Return Volatility (x-axis, 13 to 17). Two curves shown: 100% REIT and 60% Lg / 40% REIT / 100% Lg.

Source: Dimensional Fund Advisors

The shape of this chart is very different from that of the previous two. It is much flatter. This is because the annual return and the annual return volatility of these two assets classes, large U.S. stocks and REIT's are very similar. What is valuable to learn from this chart is how much the risk of having the position of 100% of either stock is reduced when you have 50% of each in the portfolio. At this point, the risk dropped from 16.5% to 13% (this is significant) and the return was no different. My conclusion is that combining real estate with large U.S. stocks gives a much lower overall portfolio return volatility. In fact, this is a better risk reducer than small U.S. stocks, which is the first diversification asset class used by most financial advisors and portfolio managers.

The data in this period showed no material difference between a 40% to 60% position in either large U.S. stocks or REIT's.

Asset Allocation Tip:
Qualified retirement plans should allocate 30% to 40% of the
U.S. large stock allocation to real estate. IRA's, personal
accounts and trusts should allocate 30% to 50% of the U.S. large
stock allocation to real estate when using REIT's, and 30% to
70% to real estate when using direct real estate investing. Move
towards a 50% allocation to real estate in your non-qualified
plans as you get closer to financial independence.

All the data for these last three charts and the following one
have been limited to the period 1978 to 2003, thus representing
only 26 years. This is because REIT data is only currently
available for that period. The previous three examples used
only two asset classes. Each incremental asset class you add has
an exponentially smaller impact on the overall portfolio. Four
or five asset classes are all one needs for full diversification.

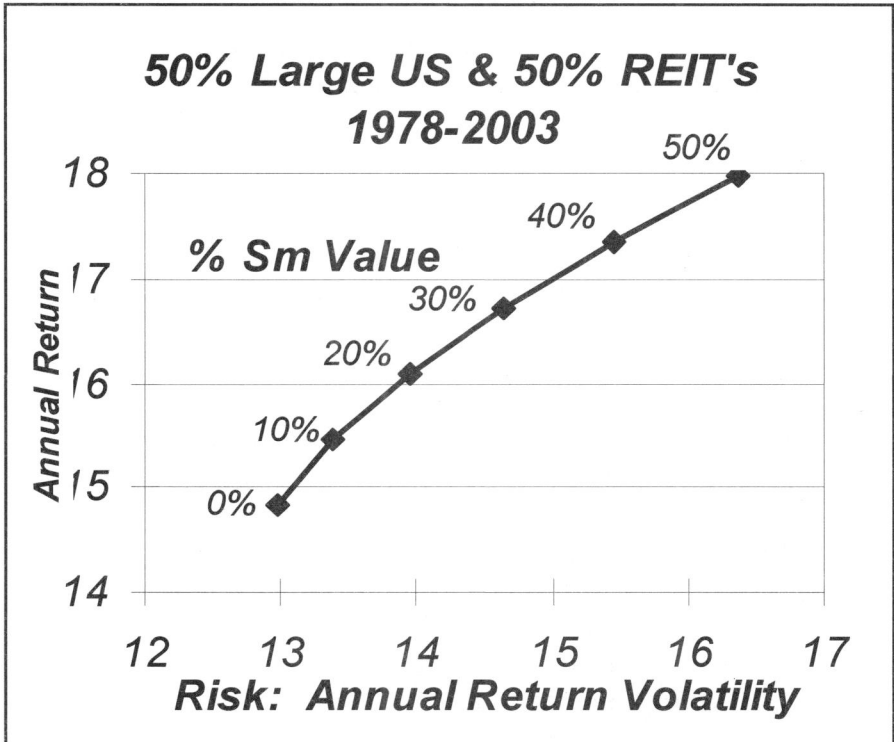

Source: Dimensional Fund Advisors

This chart uses a base portfolio of 50% large U.S. stocks and 50% of REIT's. This ratio stays constant while we add 10% to 50% small U.S. value stocks. What we see is that we get no reduction in annual return volatility by adding small U.S. value stocks. Instead, we get an increasing level of annual return volatility and an increase in annual return (at a decelerating rate).

The lack of a "hook" in this chart shows that by adding small stocks to this, already diversified, portfolio mix of large stocks and REIT's, you get proportionally more return and more risk.

My conclusion is that REIT's are your best diversification strategy. Small value stocks are a defensive addition. Keep small value stocks to between 10% and 20% of your stock allocation.

Asset Allocation Tips from this section:
- Diversify among four to five asset classes.
- Split your U.S. large stock allocation between large stocks and REIT's: a range of 30% to 40% for real estate when in a qualified plan, and 30% to 70% outside of a qualified plan.
- Keep the small stock allocation to 10% to 20% of the stock allocation.
- Use small value stocks for your small stock allocation.

Chapter 6 - Value Investing

The charts, graphs, tables and examples contained in this book are offered for purposes of illustration only. They do not imply the return that may be available on any particular investment.

Value Investing (High Book-to-Market)
In September 1991, two professors at the University of Chicago, Professor Eugene Fama and Professor Kenneth French, published a research paper titled, *Size and Book-to-Market Equity: Returns and Economic Fundamental.*

This research by Professors Fama and French broke new ground in understanding and explaining what determines returns in the stocks market. Professors Fama and French developed a three factor model to explain stock market returns over time, with a high degree of precision. The three factors are:

Factor 1 – Return Volatility (Beta).
This was the original concept developed by Professor William Sharpe, called "Beta", in which stocks with a high annual return volatility have a higher expected return over time.

Factor 2 – Company Size.
Over time, small stocks will have a higher average annual return than larger stocks. The size variable measures an additional risk dimension beyond "Beta" (return volatility).

Factor 3 – Book-to-Market.
This factor states that the book-to-market ratios of a company also contribute to explaining the annual variance in returns of stocks.

Book-to-Market:
> *Book* = Accountants' Equity (Assets minus Liabilities)
> *Market* = Stock price multiplied by the number of shares outstanding
> *Book-to-Market* = *Book* divided by *Market*
> *High book-to-market* = The 30 percentile group of companies with the highest book-to-market ratio.
> *Low book-to-market* = The 30 percentile group of companies with the lowest book-to-market ratio.

A simple way of remembering book-to-market is the accounting value (assets minus liabilities) divided by the market value (shares outstanding multiplied by the price of a share).

Re-Defining Investment Theory
Traditional investment theory, the Capital Asset Pricing Model (CAPM) states that in order to get more return you must accept more return volatility. This was a single factor model to explain the variability of individual stock returns. It does a good job by explaining 75% of the variation in returns over time. For years, this model had been the benchmark for explaining individual stock returns.

However, the three factor model does a much better job; explaining 95% of the individual variation in returns over time.

Most investment experts had no trouble understanding that the size of a company should help explain returns from stocks. Small companies are inherently more risky and, therefore, it is reasonable that this risk factor should contribute to explaining the variance in individual stock returns over time.

High book-to-market stocks are a little more complicated. High book-to-market stocks represent companies that have recently under performed. This risk factor is sometimes called the "distress factor". Why distressed companies create a return premium is not fully understood. One explanation is that buyers must be paid a premium to offset the risk that a distressed company has recently exhibited.

Investment Tip:
Active value managers nearly always under perform the full index over time. Thus, with high book-to-market investing you should use an index (statistical) approach.

Book-to-Market VS Value and Growth
High book-to-market stocks and funds are similar, but not always the same, as value stocks or value funds. High book-to-market is a rigorous mathematical way of determining if a stock is either a high or low book-to-market stock. Value stocks and value funds, on the other hand, do not always have a mathematical method of categorizing value and growth. Often funds or managers term a "value stock" whatever they deem to be "good value". Therefore, a value-fund manager will often have many low book-to-market stocks (growth stocks) in their "value" fund.

Stock reporting companies, researchers, investment professionals and investors are increasingly adopting the mathematical rigorous book-to-market definition of value and growth. The consumer should be aware that the label of "value" for a fund is still likely to hold many "growth stocks" according to a book-to-market definition. Fortunately, fund performance companies Morningstar have adopted the style box approach to indicate the overall exposure of each fund to the size and value versus growth factors on a mathematical basis.

Fama-French Return Data

U.S. High Book-to-Market Premium

1927-2003	Compound Annual Return %	1 Standard Deviation
Large U.S. Stocks		
High Book-to-Market	12.0	27.7
Full Index	10.0	20.3
Net Increase/Decrease	**2.0**	**7.4**
Small U.S. Stock		
High Book-to-Market	15.0	32.5
Full Index	12.0	31.5
Net Increase/Decrease	**3.0**	**1.0**

Source: Dimensional Fund Advisors

US Large Stocks 1927-2003
Growth of $1,000

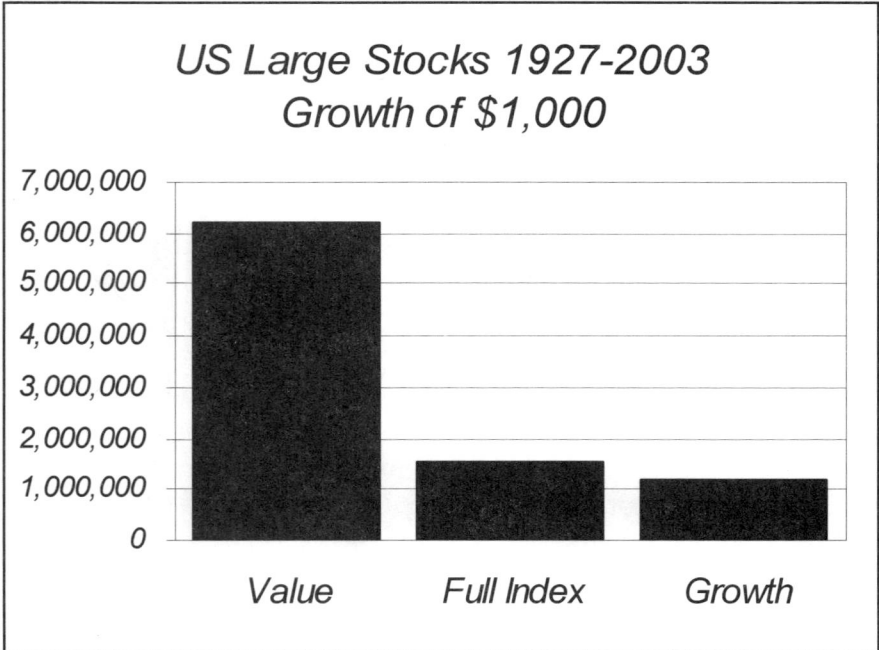

Source: Dimensional Fund Advisors

During the last 77 years, large U.S. stocks with a high book-to-market equity (value stocks) averaged 2.0% higher return per year on a compound annual return basis than the full index of large U.S. stocks. They also had more return volatility, 7.4% or 35% higher than the full index. Growth stocks under performed the full index over this same period by 0.4% a year on a compound annual return basis.

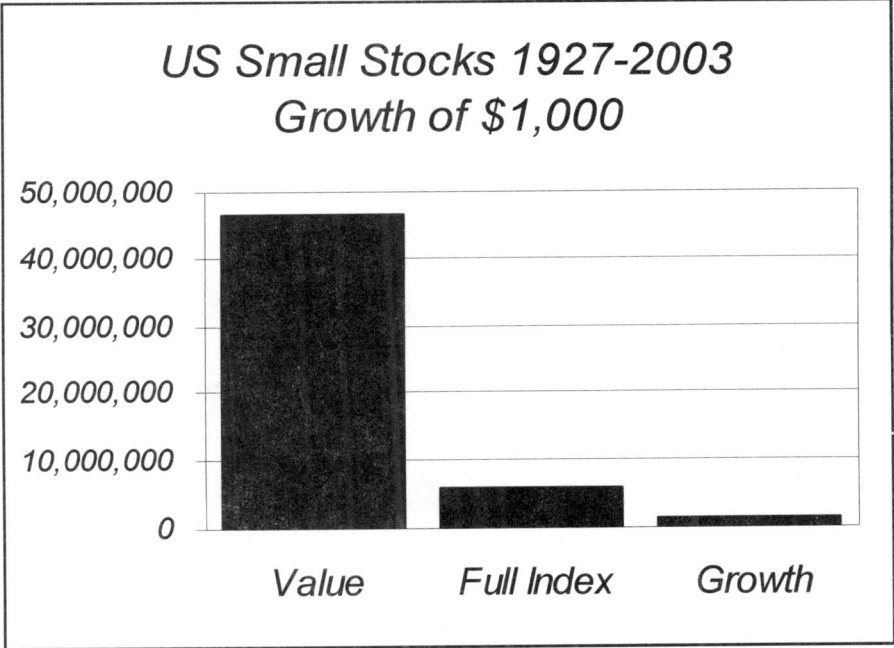

US Small Stocks 1927-2003
Growth of $1,000

[Bar chart showing Value, Full Index, and Growth bars. Y-axis ranges from 0 to 50,000,000 in increments of 10,000,000. Value bar is the tallest at approximately 45,000,000, Full Index is much smaller, and Growth is the smallest.]

Source: Dimensional Fund Advisors

Small U.S. value stocks (high book-to-market equity) averaged 3.0% higher return per year than the small stock full index over the last 77 years, on a compound annual return basis. The return volatility of small value stocks was only 1.0% per year more than the volatility for the full index over this same period.

The increased returns of high book-to-market companies over the S&P 500 and the small stock index are remarkable. Few investment managers can outperform the S&P 500 (large stock index) over 10 years. Yet, the data suggests that many should be able to, and by a significant amount, simply by investing in high book-to-market companies. Exposure to the high book-to-market risk factor should be part of all long-term investment portfolios.

Risk premiums like the book-to-market premium do not yield results each year, nor are they reliable over the medium term (3-15 years). Like stock returns versus bond returns, they are only dependable over the long term – a period greater than 15 years.

Growth versus Value (Consistency of Return Premium)
From 1927 to 2003, value stocks (high book-to-market) did not always outperform growth stocks (low book-to-market).

Two charts each are presented for both large stocks and for small stocks. The first chart in each sequence shows the average annual returns of value stocks minus growth stocks. The second in each sequence shows the ten-year average annual return of value minus growth.

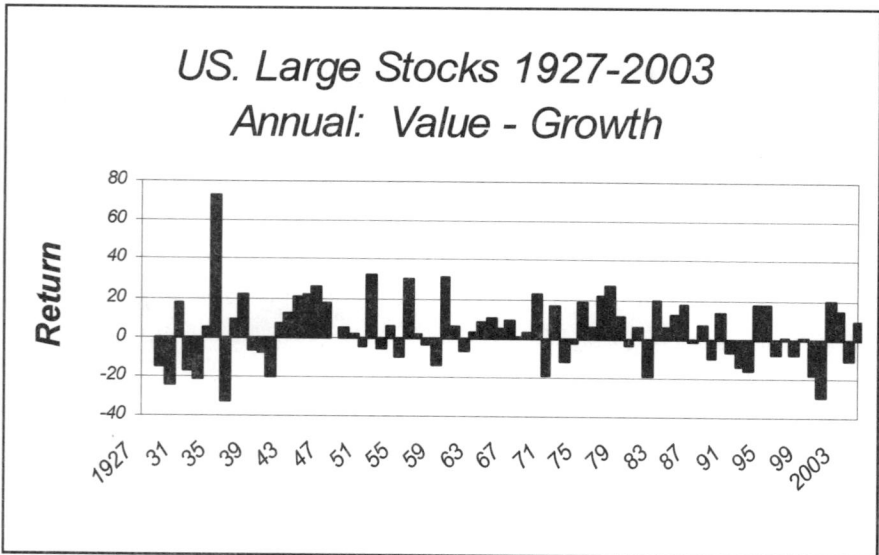

US. Large Stocks 1927-2003
Annual: Value - Growth

Source: Dimensional Fund Advisors

This chart for large U.S. stocks shows that value regularly outperforms growth, but not always; growth can certainly have its turn at superior performance.

US. Large Stocks 1927-2003
10 Year Avg: Value - Growth

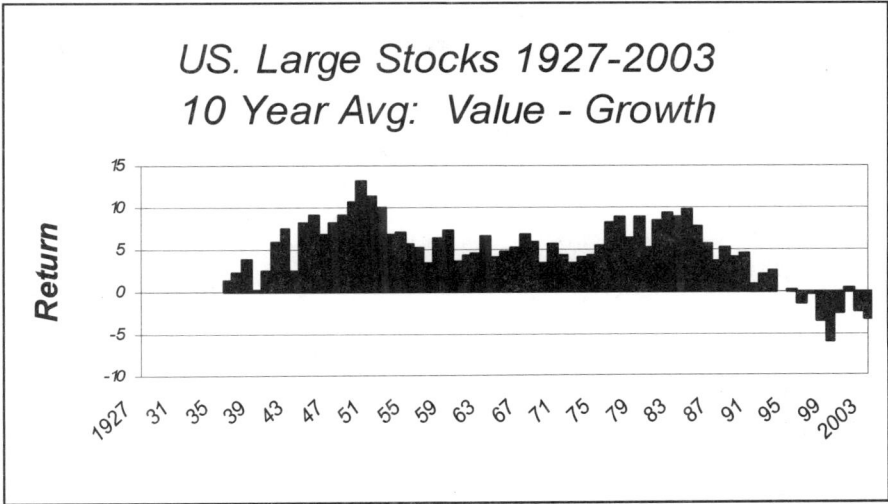

Source: Dimensional Fund Advisors

This chart shows that with large U.S. stocks, even over a ten-year period, value does not always outperform growth. In fact, the rolling ten-year averages of late have seen periods where growth has outperformed value. This irregularity demonstrates the challenge in embracing the value premium. Like the stock premium and the size premium, the value premium can take more than ten years to capture. Thus, diversification is necessary in your portfolio design, while keeping some exposure to value in favor of growth.

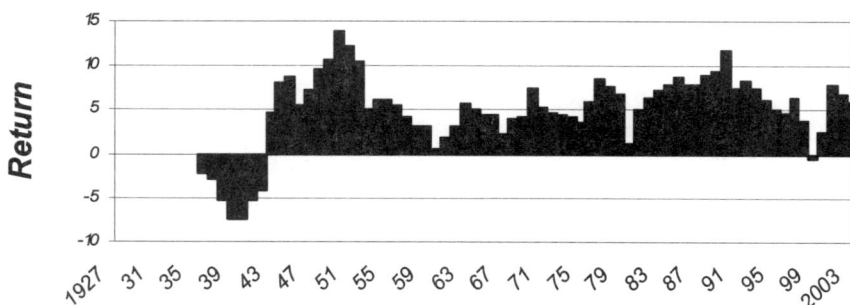

US. Small Stocks 1927-2003
10 Year Avg: Value - Growth

Source: Dimensional Fund Advisors

This chart shows the ten-year average difference in return for value minus growth for U.S. small stocks. Two things stand out in this graph. First, the annual average benefit from value stocks over ten years is often considerable – more than 5%. Second, there still can be ten-year periods of time when small growth stocks outperform small value stocks, but not by more than 5%, and not very often.

Asset Allocation Tip:
When building an asset allocation portfolio the allocation to small U.S. stocks and to small international stocks can be as much as 100% in value. We recommend against using growth in your small stock allocation, as it underperforms by a substantial amount over time compared to the full index and to value.

International High Book-to-Market Effect
A study entitled *International Value and Growth Stock Returns* by Carlo Capaul, Ian Rowley and Nobel Prize Laureate, Professor William Sharpe *(Financial Analysts Journal*, February 1993), and another by John R. Chisolm both concluded that the book-to-market effect is also statistically significant for all major international markets.

In the Chisolm study, the average difference in annual compound returns between high and low book-to-market stocks was 8.35%.

In late 1993, Professors Fama and French looked at the international book-to-market stock data on a country by country basis. Their review covered all 13 EAFE (Europe, Asia, and Far East) countries for the 18-year period ending December 31, 1992. The results were consistent with those found in the United States; book-to-market risk characteristics are statistically significant. This is an important finding because this is considered an out-of-sample verification of the longer-term U.S. data on the book-to-market risk premium.

The EAFE large company (net of dividends) high book-to-market premium over the EAFE full index (net of dividends) has been 2.0% over the last 29 years on a compound return basis.

This increase in return occurred with no measurable increase in the volatility of annual return.

International Large Stocks
High Book-to-Market (Net of Dividends)

1975-2003

	Compound Annualized Return	Annual Return Volatility – 1 Std. Dev.
High Book-to-Market EAFE	13.9	22.1
EAFE	11.9	21.9
Difference	2.0	0.2

Source: Dimensional Fund Advisors

In a 10-year study by Professor Kenneth French (1997) on the book-to-market risk factor within the Emerging Markets, the "value" segment substantially outperformed the full index, with a modest increase in volatility.

A common question we get is, "what will happen to these historical relationships when everyone else finds out about them"? The answer is – nothing. Knowledge of the stock to bond premium (return volatility) did not eliminate or reduce the stock premium. Knowledge of the size premium did not reduce the size premium. The distress premium will remain, even when it is broadly accepted as a risk premium.

Nothing truly valuable arises from ambition or from a mere sense of duty; it stems rather from love and devotion towards men and towards objective things.

- Albert Einstein

CHAPTER 7 - International Stocks

The charts, graphs, tables, and examples contained in this book are offered for purposes of illustration only. They do not imply the return that may be available on any particular investment.

Global Diversification

Today, we are in a unique economic time in history. We have completed the first round of industrialization, with Japan, and the tiger economies of South East Asia joining the industrialized world. Meanwhile, the emerging markets of China, India, the other nations in South East Asia, South America, Africa, Russia, and most of the former eastern European countries are still industrializing. The last forty years were an economic boom period during which America and industrialized Europe exported their industrial knowledge around the world. Labor costs dropped dramatically as production shifted to low labor-cost nations. This, in turn, fueled unprecedented profits for international conglomerates.

Today these same multinational companies are exporting service jobs from the U.S. to India. This is generating another round of profits for multinational companies from reduced labor costs. Both the manufacturing and the service jobs are a once in a life time economic opportunity. These events are changing the world and connecting it in ways we could not have imagined even 15 years ago.

Your investments should include both large and small international companies, and the emerging markets for the benefit of geographic diversification.

U.S. & International Stock Returns

	Annual Compound Return	Annual Return Volatility
1970-2003 (34 Years)		
U.S. Large Stock	11.1	17.9
Int'l Large Stocks	13.0	26.5
U.S. Small Stocks	12.6	24.5
Int'l Small Stocks	16.0	30.5
1994-2003 (10 Years)		
U.S. Large Stocks	10.7	21.8
Int'l Large Stocks	4.4	20.8
U.S. Small Stocks	12.7	23.8
Int'l Small Stocks	4.3	22.2

Large Stocks
U.S. & International
1970 - 2003 (34 Yrs)

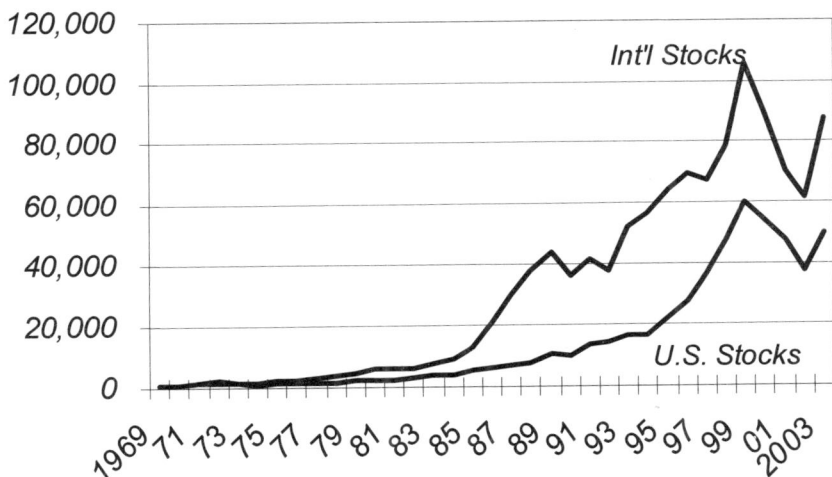

Source: Dimensional Fund Advisors

Over the last 34 years ending December 31, 2003 (the longest period for which full index data are available for the international stock markets), large international stocks have outperformed large U.S. stocks by 1.9% (13.0% vs.11.1%) on a compound annual-return basis. However, international stocks had 48% more volatility during that same time.

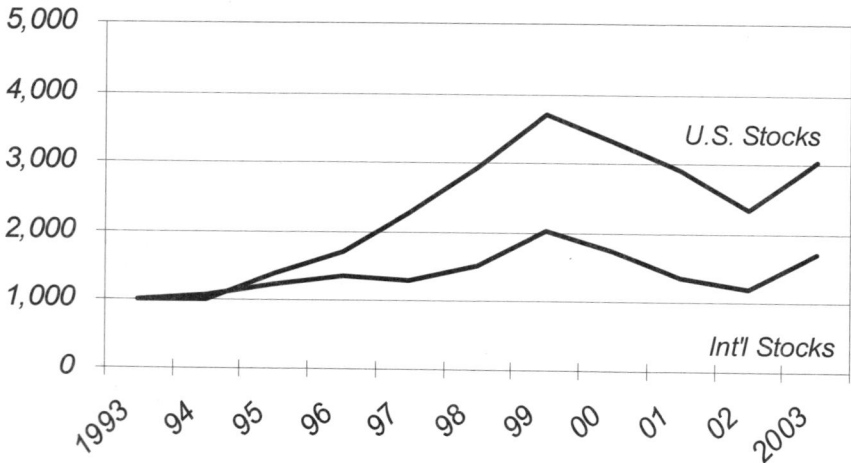

**Large Stocks
U.S. & International
1994 - 2003 (10 Yrs)**

U.S. Stocks

Int'l Stocks

Source: Dimensional Fund Advisors

Over the last 10 years, U.S. large stocks have outperformed international large stocks.

Small Stocks
U.S. & International
1970 - 2003 (34 Yrs)

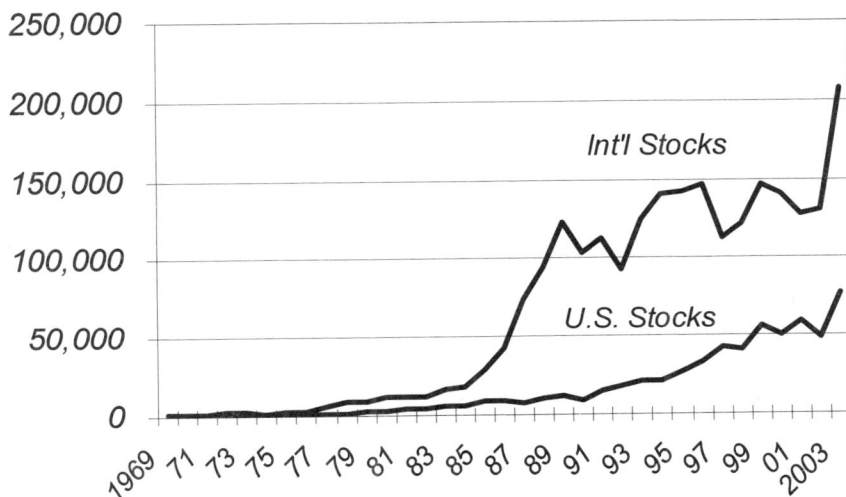

Source: Dimensional Fund Advisors

Small international stocks also outperformed small U.S. stocks by 3.4% a year (16.0% vs. 12.6%) on a compound annual-return basis. However, international small stocks had 25% more annual volatility than U.S. small stocks in that same period.

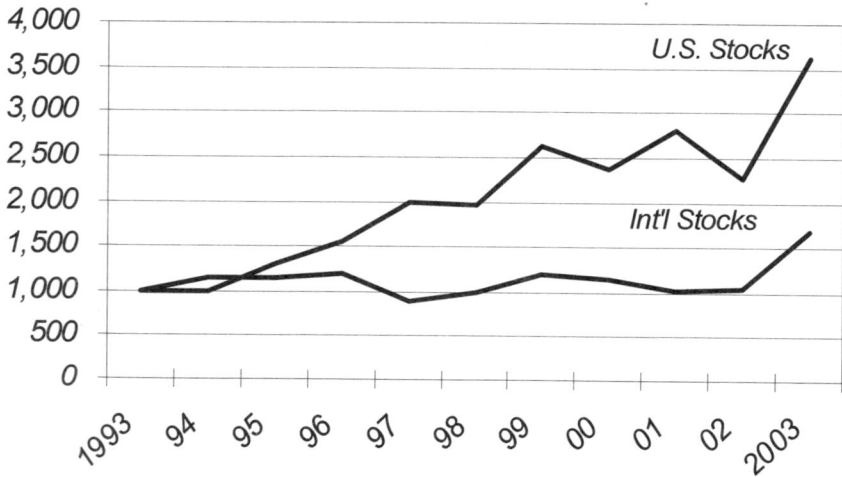

Small Stocks
U.S. & International
1994 - 2003 (10 Yrs)

U.S. Stocks

Int'l Stocks

Source: Dimensional Fund Advisors

Over the last 10 years, U.S. small stocks have outperformed international small stocks.

Because of the cross correlation effect (where the stock gains and losses occur at different times for the U.S. and international markets), including international stocks in your portfolio can both increase overall long-term returns, and reduce volatility. International stocks and international value stocks belong in your long-term investment portfolio.

To summarize:
International stocks have been more volatile than U.S. stocks, and most of their modest additional return can be attributed to this increased return volatility. Over the long haul, there is no reason to believe that international stock compound annual returns will be materially different from U.S. returns.

World's Stock Markets
The main two reasons for including international stocks in your asset allocation are:

Cross-Correlation / Diversification Benefits
Because each country has unique business cycles, including international stocks in your portfolio can reduce its overall return volatility.

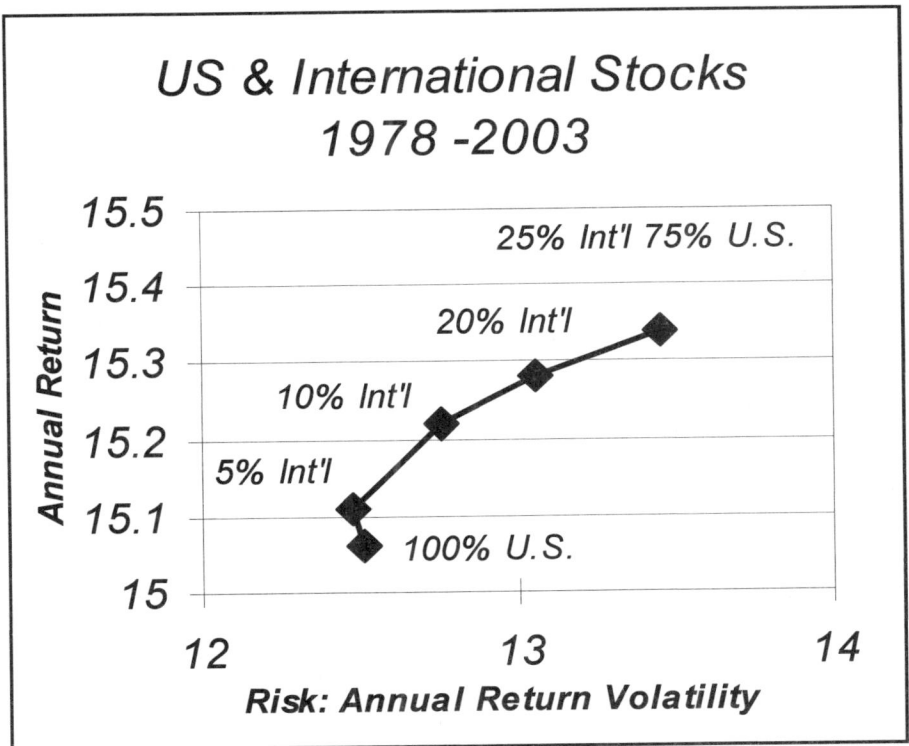

US & International Stocks
1978 -2003

Annual Return

25% Int'l 75% U.S.

20% Int'l

10% Int'l

5% Int'l

100% U.S.

15.5 · 15.4 · 15.3 · 15.2 · 15.1 · 15

12 · 13 · 14

Risk: Annual Return Volatility

Source: Dimensional Fund Advisors

This chart shows what happens when you start with a balanced U.S. all stock portfolio – made up of 35% large U.S. stock, 35% REIT's, and 30% U.S. small value stocks. We then added 5% international stocks (split 70% to large, and 30% to small). As you can see, the first 5% we added reduced portfolio volatility while increasing return. As we introduced more international stocks, both return and volatility increased by modest amounts. Reducing return volatility to a three asset class, well-diversified portfolio was difficult to do, especially when using a more volatile asset class.

Defensive Strategy:
The use of international stocks in a portfolio design is defensive for the periods when international stocks outperform U.S. stocks, rather than for meaningful portfolio risk reduction. It is far better to have some ongoing meaningful exposure to international stocks, rather than to only switch some of your allocation after international stocks have already begun their run against U.S. stocks.

Asset Allocation Tip:
Allocate between 10% and 25% of your stocks to international stocks.

Emerging Markets
The transition of more than 60% of the world's population from communist and socialist economies to capitalist-based economies is one of the most significant economic events in history. In 2003, we are in the middle stages of this unprecedented economic event.

The implementation of Western technology in these economies will continue to be rapid and should lead to major leaps in prosperity. The West still has much of its industrial technology yet to be shared with the emerging markets; and they, in turn, can provide labor at substantial savings.

Over the next two to three decades, the world will change more than at any other time in history, in part because of the implementation of existing western technology in the previously undeveloped nations of China, India, Indonesia, and

Russia, which, together, represent more than one half of today's world population.

Japan, Taiwan, South Korea, Hong Kong, and Singapore have created the most successful blueprints for this change; and the world's investors are eager to provide capital, as long as they have political stability and a fair game. For multinational corporations, the supply of reasonably well educated labor at low cost is a real boon to corporate profits.

The following table shows the returns of the emerging market's large stock asset class over the maximum period data has been available.

1988 – 2003		
	Annualized %	Annual Return Volatility
U.S. Large Stocks	12.4%	18.8%
Emerging Market	16.8%	45.1%
U.S. Small Stocks	13.9%	22.5%

Source: Dimensional Fund Advisors

This last table shows that the emerging market asset class returned more than large U.S. stocks and small U.S. stocks for the same period. It has to be stressed, however, that the maximum period for which we have comparable data is quite short at 16 years. What is more important to notice is that it does so with a very high amount of annual return volatility compared to either large or small U.S. stocks. As such, the inclusion of emerging market funds in your portfolio is truly optional. A more high risk investor may seek to add this asset class, but should do so in a conservative manner, and only with a very long-term time horizon.

20% International Portfolio 1988 -2002

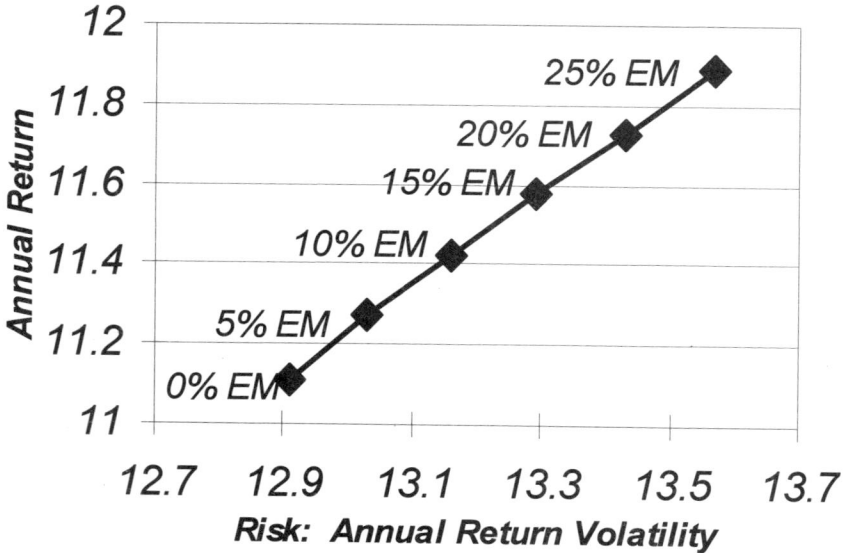

Source: Dimensional Fund Advisors

This graph starts with a base portfolio of 20% International stock from our earlier diversified portfolio. It has 30% in large U.S. stocks 30% in REIT, 20% in small U.S. value stock, 15% in large International stock, 5% in small international stocks, and 0% in emerging market stocks. We then increase the exposure of emerging market stocks as a percentage of the total international stock allocation, in 5% increments. The resulting graph shows a similar pattern of no risk reduction, but increased return with increased return volatility.

Because emerging market stocks have a high return volatility, we recommend only a very small allocation to this asset class in your overall portfolio. The allocation to the emerging markets should be a portion of your international allocation; 15% to 20% would be a reasonable amount.

Chapter 8 - Real Estate

The charts, graphs, tables, and examples contained in this book are offered for purposes of illustration only. They do not imply the return that may be available on any particular investment.

There are two forms of real estate ownership for investment purposes – individual holdings and Real Estate Investment Trusts (REIT's). Each method has its unique characteristics, and accompanying advantages and disadvantages.

Real estate is the largest pool of investment assets held in America; in fact, it is three times larger than the value of the U.S. stock market.

Real estate has gone through recent challenges as an investment class. From the 1970s through to the mid 1980s, real estate limited partnerships were the most widely marketed investment vehicle. This came to an abrupt halt with the curbing of tax shelter abuses via the Tax Reform Act of 1986. Since the second half of the 1980's stocks and stock mutual funds have dominated the purchases of most investment managers and individual investors.

Financial planners, mutual fund investment advisors and trust departments all followed this trend. Over the last fifteen years investment portfolio allocation practice has treated real estate investing as an "alternative investment" asset class. Currently, other alternative investments include commodities (metals, oil and gas, raw materials), options and futures, and collectibles (paintings, coins, cars, stamps, Chinese pottery and too many other rare and collectible items to mention).

Alternative investments are limited in the role they play in the overall portfolio for safety reasons (Prudent Investor Rules, and the Broker Dealer rules of individual investment advisors). The labeling of real estate investing as an alternative investment was in our opinion an overreaction to the IRS crackdown on tax shelter abuses. Land is one asset class within real estate that does fit into the "alternative investment" category.

The biggest concern about real estate as an investment is its lack of liquidity. This, however, is simply another risk factor and one that you are paid, in the marketplace, to bear.

There are two significant advantages in favor of including real estate in your overall portfolio. Firstly, real estate is one of the best asset classes to diversify against large U.S. stocks. Secondly, because real estate is difficult to sell in a down market, it forces the owner to have more discipline and to manage the asset through most recessions, rather than sell it off at its lowest value, as is often done with poor performing stocks and mutual funds.

Real estate is a real, rather than a paper, asset. Real estate leases are typically of medium term and provide a known income for a fixed number of years, with the income often being inflation adjusted. Even when businesses declare bankruptcy or default on their bond obligations, most do not abandon the majority of their real estate leases, as they need places to operate. It is difficult to move and incur remodeling costs when you are already cash strapped.

Real Estate Investment Trusts (REIT's)
These are real estate funds that possess many properties. Typically, they are well diversified as to both region and type of holding. Most REIT's have little or no debt on their properties. They have a very high distribution rate, in fact, the highest distribution rate of any mutual fund type. The distribution rate as of 12-31-2002 for the Vanguard REIT was 6.4%, according to Morningstar. Conversely, the 10-year

Treasury rate was only around 6.0% as of 12-31-2002, and it had no price appreciation potential, as did the REIT.

Since REIT's are mutual funds, they are available for purchase and sale on a daily basis just like any mutual fund.

1978 - 2003

	Compound Annual Return	Annual Return Volatility
U.S. Large Stocks	13.4%	16.4%
REIT – Wilshire Index	13.8%	16.7%

Source: Dimensional Fund Advisors

The table above and the chart that follows show that over the last 26 years (maximum period data is available) REIT's have had a compound annual return comparable to U.S. large stocks. The volatility was also similar over this same period. REIT's and large stocks tend to be on different business cycles from time to time.

Twenty-six years of data is a sufficient amount of time to compare the return volatility of these two asset classes and their cross-correlation coefficient. It is too short, however, for reliable long term annual return comparison. It is my guess that over a longer time frame, U.S. large stocks, with their much lower current income rate (dividends) and higher price appreciation, should have a slight total return advantage over real estate, perhaps in the 1.0% range.

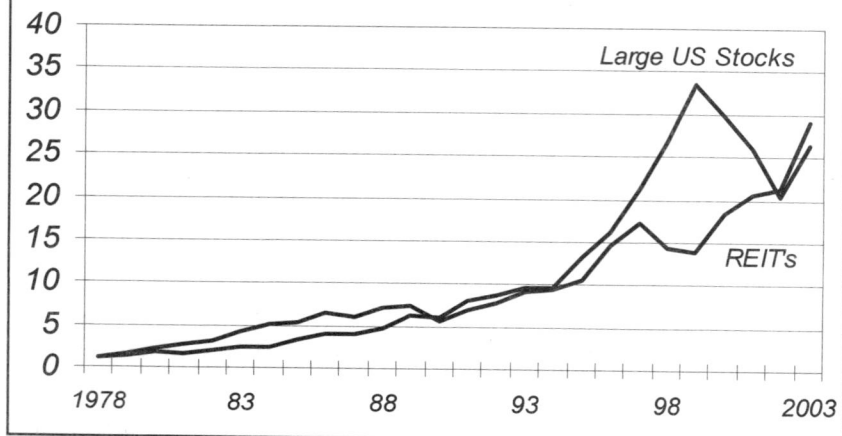

**REIT's VS Large U.S. Stocks
Growth of $1
1978 - 2003**

Source: Dimensional Fund Advisors

Most financial advisors recommend little or no allocation to REIT's and nearly always no direct real estate holdings. I think this is a significant mistake, brought about by an overreaction to the tax shelter abuses in the 1980s and the subsequent labeling of real estate as an alternative investment.

When you buy a REIT, you essentially own a real estate based stock. When the stock price of the REIT declines, it is easy for you to sell. Thus, the ready market of a REIT comes with a cost. You lose the powerful direct experience of your real estate income remaining steady, even during most recessions. Of course, the high dividend rate of the REIT is a ready substitute for the tangible experience of stable rental income in the early stages of an economic slowdown.

Direct Real Estate Investing
Direct real estate investing has some advantages and some disadvantages. The unique aspect of direct real estate investing is that it takes a very large up front investment to participate.

84

Thus, direct real estate investing is not for everyone. It is, in our opinion, very appropriate for larger private trusts, an area in which they are generally not very active at the present time.

Most direct real estate investment is done with a 30% down payment with the balance paid via a loan. This loan is a systematic reinvestment program. Most commercial loans are amortized over 20 or 25 years. The systematic pay down of principal is a "Pay Yourself First" program.

Perhaps the best aspect of direct real estate investing is the discipline it brings, which helps one to behave as a successful long-term investor. This is because with real estate, there are both high transaction costs involved in selling, and difficulty in selling investment real estate in a weak market.

This lack of marketability combined with an investor's aversion to loss will drive many investors to ride out price declines. Often, this is the best course of action, as long as the underlying economy is expected to recover.

With direct real estate ownership, you are in control. This is most helpful when you are trying to determine if you are financially independent and if you will outlast your money. When direct real estate investing makes up a substantial portion of your portfolio it is easier to recognize whether or not you are financially independent. This is because with real estate you experience your rental leases, and know that they have built-in, annual inflation escalation clauses. You also experience that the underlying value of the real estate goes through steady long term appreciation. Thus, with direct real estate investment, if you have enough Passive Income to meet your current life-style needs, you should be able to maintain this same life-style for the rest of your life without having to save or add to your assets.

Direct real estate investing also has a unique advantage for estate planning. It is the income that we need for financial independence, not the ownership of the underlying assets. Through the use of a Family Limited Partnership and a GRAT it is possible to utilize the income for both you and your partner's lives, control the underlying asset, transfer the underlying asset out of your estate (for around one half of its present value), and keep all future appreciation out of your estate.

Unique Characteristics of Real Estate

Easier to be a Successful Long-Term Investor

Even a novice real estate investor acts more like a long-term investor and less like a reactionary investor when prices of real estate fall (as opposed to when prices of stocks fall). The lessons learned from successful real estate investing teaches individuals to use more restraint with their stock investments. Most investors go through a period of learning from their mistakes. The mistakes associated with real estate have more to do with maintenance, tenant issues, and cash flow management than with selling at the wrong time due to an over reaction to a price decline.

Leverage

Leverage lets you purchase an asset of greater value than you have cash to invest. Thus, a $300,000 investment can be used to acquire a $1,000,000 asset. If the $1,000,000 asset goes up by 10% the next year, your equity grows by $100,000. Based on a $300,000 investment, your investment grew that year by 33%. Of course, leverage can work both ways.

Inefficient Market

Not all real estate within a country, state, county or city appreciates at the same rate.

Unlike stocks, we believe that with real estate it is possible to identify where it is most likely to grow at a faster rate over the medium to long term.

For example, beach-front property near a major business center is likely to experience sustained above average growth.

Land and buildings in and near a robust business center would be expected to experience sustained above average growth.

The rules for this superior real estate appreciation are straight forward. There are, however, complicating factors in any situation that can counteract future estimates. For example, when defense spending took a dive in the early 1990s, southern California experienced a 25% setback in real estate prices, substantial office vacancies, and job losses – something it had been almost immune to for decades. The economy subsequently diversified and absorbed the job losses. Soon Los Angeles and the surrounding communities returned to above average growth and its real estate prices began rising at a steady rate again.

The Past 40 Years – The Next 40 years

From the late 1950's through to today, the industrialized nations have been busy bringing technology to developing nations. In exchange, multinational corporations were able to reduce their labor costs and make more profit. This process moved steadily from nation to nation. Today, the last major sources of cheap labor, China and India, are well into this process. The largest of the cost reductions from this process are now behind us. Unit labor costs will slowly rise from now on. The deflation in product costs we have grown accustomed to over the last thirty years are likely to lessen as labor gets progressively more expensive.

The growth in stock values over the last 20 years has been especially robust. This solid run of good corporate profits was in large part fueled by the process of exporting production to lower-cost labor markets.

The next 40 years is, of course, impossible to predict with certainty. However, analysis of some fundamental factors can give us a clue as to how the next forty years are likely to be different.

The internet and high speed data cable has allowed services like U.S. loan processing and U.S. technical support to be performed in places like India. This brings the world closer together and speeds up economic activity.

We know that a very large pool of consumers is steadily developing in China. One third of the world's population lives in China and India. Over time, their standard of living will expand and they will demand more consumer products and services. This will support more economic activity. The pace of this change is faster than anyone ever imagined.

Slowly, wages in the developing countries will rise to reach a relative parity with the rest of the developed world. This process will be a steady drag on the profits of the world's largest companies; conversely, however, the new consumers will be a plus for business growth.

We have all seen how advances in technology and communication are bringing the world's cultures closer together. The rate of change from established technology implementation is slowing, whereas the rate of change from new technology continues to increase at a geometric rate.

There are other major trends evolving that will shape the future. The world's population continues to grow at an alarming rate, especially in third-world countries. Water is becoming increasingly scarce in most industrialized areas. Energy drives both the industrialized world and the information age. Break-through advances in energy supply, such as from fuel cells, could bring about a significant onetime windfall for modern business. More and more consumers around the world want the abundance enjoyed by industrialized economies.

Quality of life issues are increasing in importance as cities become more crowded, freeways more clogged, and new technologies enable us to work remotely from the corporate center. This points to an increasing demand for choice real estate both concentrated around major business centers and in areas of better climate and nearer to recreation areas.

The next forty years are likely to be a prime period for real estate, just as the last forty years were a prime period for multinational businesses. Just how good the profits will be is hard to say. Where the biggest winners are likely to be is much easier to define.

Conditions for above Average Real Estate Returns
It is possible, with a high degree of confidence, to predict where real estate will appreciate faster than average over the medium to long term. It is not as easy to identify bubbles that occur in overheated real estate markets, which can be a setback to long term superior growth.

Factor 1: Strong Business Growth
Strong business growth occurs reliably where there is the most freedom and a strong and adaptive infrastructure. It also occurs in the short run where a new technology is introduced. The more diversified an area is, the better its ability to survive and prosper uninterrupted over time.

The U.S. has shown its ability to succeed at sustained business growth better than most nations today. It is likely to be able to continue this growth record, and to be one of the more stable world economies because of its broad diversification and high levels of personal freedom.

My personal favorite economy for real estate investing is Singapore. It has excellent freedoms, outstanding infrastructure, and its small size is also advantageous. It is like taking New York, teaching it to act like Switzerland, and having it reclassified as a country. Unfortunately, foreigners cannot directly own Singapore real estate if it's below the sixth floor. I am a little biased as this is where I grew up.

Factor 2: Scarcity of New Development Opportunities
A scarcity of new real estate development opportunities is necessary for values and rents to appreciate faster than costs are rising. Often real estate growth is limited by geographic constraints such as the size of a valley. Another constraint can be transportation systems. The better the transportation system the more room there is for growth in distance from the main business centers. Water is often another constraint on land development. Sometimes a particular community will adopt slow growth policies capping the number of permits allowed each year.

Individual ownership of real estate also has its disadvantages

Real Estate is Expensive to Purchase
Real estate investing requires saving for many months, and sometimes years, before a purchase can be made.

Leverage Can Work Against You
Real estate is leveraged, and leverage can work for you or against you. Over time, on balance, it works for you. Occasionally it will go against you. With real estate, you can lose more than your initial investment. Such an example occurred in Texas in the late 1980s when oil prices collapsed. Real estate prices dropped for many years, and vacancy rates soared. The closer to the edge you play it, the more risk real estate has. If you have a good cash reserve, you can survive long term recessions. A large cash reserve is more important than little or no leverage.

Real Estate Requires Management
You can, of course, hire this out, but it is essential that you take good care of your properties and perform your required maintenance. As the car mechanic said, "You can pay me a little now, or a lot later". Failure to perform required maintenance could also negatively affect your tenant relationships.

You Can Get Sued
When you own a building, you can get sued. This does not happen when you own a stock. Therefore, when you own real estate, you need good insurance coverage.

Lack of Diversification
The best cure for many of the risks associated with real estate is diversification. If you have only one tenant then your cash flow risk rides with that tenant. If you have 10 equal sized tenants and one leaves, you have a minor inconvenience. If you have one tenant that occupies more than 30% of any building, then you should increase their security deposit and be sure you are comfortable with that company and their industry. Having all your real estate in one geographic region is a business risk. But it is one that can be mitigated by being in a location that has good business diversity and strong economic fundamentals.

Vacancies

In the short run, unforeseen vacancies in individual real estate can be a problem. With residential real estate, this is less of a concern than it is with commercial or industrial real estate. In a recession, it can be difficult and costly to find a commercial tenant. Thus, you must have tenant diversification and cash reserves. During a recession, people still need a place to live. It simply may take a rent concession to get a tenant. The one major exception to this would be a town that has lost its primary employer.

The Value of Income Stability

A high rate of income, combined with stability of this income, is the Promised Land for a retired person. If you add the ability of both this income and the underlying asset, to grow at, or above, the inflation rate, you have a very valuable long term asset. Real estate is a preferred asset to hold in a long-term family trust. As the dogma of seeing real estate as an "alternative investment" wears off, trust departments and trustees will eventually warm to this concept. You do not have to wait, however. Instead, just demand that this be done with 30% to 50% of your assets. Ten years from now you should be very pleased that you did.

The greater the need to provide income from a portfolio, the more beneficial it is to add real estate holdings to a portfolio.

In Summary:

Real estate investing (REIT's and direct real estate) should form a substantial basis of most investment portfolios. The real estate asset class is one of the best ways to diversify large stocks in a portfolio. Real estate investing, because of its permanent nature, provides better long-term discipline to the investment process, particularly direct real estate investing. Real estate provides a high current income that appreciates at, or ahead of, the inflation rate over the long term, while the underlying asset value also appreciates similarly. It is easy for investors and beneficiaries of a trust to understand how real estate will provide the income they need for financial independence, both today and into the future, without having to consume principal. Direct real estate investment is a good estate-planning asset.

Loans on direct real estate investments provide a systematic reinvestment program that builds capital over time. Real estate is an efficient asset, and above average returns are possible for sustained periods. The next 30 years look promising for real estate investment.

Asset Allocation Tip:
Qualified retirement plans can allocate 30% to 40% of the U.S. large stock allocation to real estate. IRAs, personal accounts and trusts can allocate 30% to 50% of the U.S. large stock allocation to real estate when using REIT's, and 30% to 70% to real estate when using direct real estate investing. Move towards a 50% allocation to real estate in your non-qualified plans as you get closer to financial independence.

Chapter 9 - Portfolio Design

The charts, graphs, tables, and examples contained in this book are offered for purposes of illustration only. They do not imply the return that may be available on any particular investment.

Portfolio Design Criteria
As previously explained, portfolio design is the most important determinant of return in your portfolio, accounting for at least 90% of the return each year. As such, portfolio design is the area you should put most of your time and effort into.

Portfolio design is unique for each investment portfolio. The allocation you use with a college fund is not the same allocation you will use with your retirement funds. The art and science of portfolio design, asset classification, and investment instruments are constantly evolving.

Financial planners can help employers develop, maintain, and implement written portfolio design statements that meet their fiduciary requirements when they have employees in a qualified plan.

The emphasis of the investment section of this book has been on how to implement the concepts presented into the portfolio design, because this is what really matters when investing.

Portfolio Design Approach

The following is a typical approach used by financial planners in assisting clients with their portfolio design decisions.

Step 1: Define the time horizon of each account. This often requires the use of financial planning software to develop an overall financial independence strategy.

Step 2: Define the risk tolerance level of each account.

Step 3: Choose the percentage of stock, real estate and bonds for the overall portfolio.

Step 4: Decide on the allocation of stock to go to the international and emerging markets.

Step 5: Decide how to allocate each of the stocks asset classes between the style choices of full index, value and growth.

Step 6: Decide on the maximum allocation to highly speculative asset classes like collectibles, closely held stocks, close-friends-can't-miss deals, raw land, or in stocks with prices less than $5.00.

Step 7: Put this asset allocation policy in writing.

Step 8: Follow this plan.

Step 9: Review this policy at least every two years with your financial advisor or your investment committee.

Investment Implementation

Once you choose a portfolio design, your next step is to choose how to fund it. Your stock choices are individual stocks, mutual funds or ETFs. With real estate, your choices are direct ownership or REITs.

Mutual funds and ETFs are the best solution. With mutual funds you have to choose between those that are actively managed or an index or statistical approach. Our preferences have been explained earlier for each of the various asset classes.

Benchmark Measurement

At least once a year, the performance of each fund in your portfolio needs to be benchmarked against the return of the asset class it comprises, in order to properly monitor the fund's performance and adherence to that asset class. If you use a financial advisor, they should do this for you.

The decile rating system is used to statistically define asset classes. The deciles system was developed by the Center for Research in Security Prices (CRSP) who provide much of the long term historical data used by researchers. The system works as follows: If you take the entire universe of all 9,000+ stocks in the U.S. and rank them by size (shares outstanding multiplied by market price), you then can divide these stocks into ten groups of 900 stocks, each ranked by size. If a particular stock is in the largest group, it is called a decile 1 stock. If a stock is one of the 900 smallest stocks, it is a decile 10 stock.

The same thing is done with ranking stocks by their book-to-market (BtM) ratios. All 9,000+ are rated and then separated into one of ten decile groups. Those with the highest BtM ratio are decile 1 and those with the lowest, decile 10.

The primary stock market benchmark indexes include:

Large U.S. Stocks:
    Dow Jones Industrial Average (DJIA)
    S&P 500
    Full Index - size deciles 1-5
    Value - size deciles 1-5 & BtM decile 1-3
    Growth – size deciles 1-5 & BtM deciles 8-10

Small U.S. Stocks:
    Schwab 2000
    Full Index - size deciles 6-10
    Value - size deciles 6-10 & BtM deciles 1-3
    Growth – size deciles 6-10 & BtM deciles 8-10

International Large Stocks: EAFE Large Companies Index

International Small Stocks: EAFE Small Companies Index

Emerging Market Stocks: Emerging Market Index

Note: BtM stands for Book-to-Market.

The NASDAQ 1000 index is not presented here as an asset class index as it contains both large and small stocks. It is a composite of 1000 stocks from the technology laden NASDAQ exchange, which includes companies from the DJIA as well as some of the smallest stocks in the U.S. stock market.

Rating services such as Morningstar have recognized the need to measure fund performance against the appropriate benchmark. You too should measure the individual performance of each of your funds against the appropriate benchmark. This is the best way to determine if your fund is staying within its asset class. It also helps you measure the performance of the fund manager.

Too often investors measure the performance of all stock mutual funds against only the DJIA index or the S&P 500 index. This is incorrect, and in essence says that diversification and portfolio design are invalid. Since the diversification in your portfolio design is the most important determinant of return, it follows that measuring your fund choices against the appropriate benchmark is what is appropriate.

Bonds in a Portfolio Design
The primary purpose of bonds in a portfolio is to mitigate volatility because higher returns are most efficiently achieved through stocks and real estate. For this reason, taxable bonds in a portfolio design should be short-term (1-2 year average maturity) and of high quality, either Treasury grade or investment grade corporate bonds. In a taxable account, the average maturity should be 3-5 years.

For portfolio investing, the bond funds should be short-term and high investment grade only. Vanguard and other major mutual fund providers have excellent low-fee retail choices for both short-term taxable and tax-free bond funds.

For taxable accounts, use either a state-specific municipal bond fund or an all-state bond fund. Municipal bond funds used in your personal portfolio should have a little longer average maturity due to the difference in the municipal bond yield curve over the taxable bond yield curve. The municipal bond short-term fund should have an average maturity of no more than 5 years. With tax-free bonds, the yield curve does not begin to flatten out until around the 4- or 5-year range. The taxable bond yield curve typically starts to flatten out around the1- or 2-year range.

Portfolio Designs
There is no one perfect portfolio design. Nor are there a series of perfect portfolio designs for you to choose from. A portfolio design is a reasonable guideline of how to diversify your investment portfolio. If you went to 1,000 financial planners, you would be likely to get 1,000 unique portfolio designs.

Large versus Small Stocks
The overall stock market is made up of 70% large stocks and 30% small stocks. Small stocks have more annual return volatility than large stocks. The potential for long periods of under performance is what drives people out of small stocks over time. I believe that high BtM small stocks offer a superior way to own small stocks in a balanced portfolio. I recommend an allocation of 15% to 30% of stocks to small stocks, based on your overall risk tolerance.

International Stocks
The primary reason for including international stocks in a U.S. investor's portfolio is for the diversification benefits. As such, I recommend you allocate 10% to 25% of your stock allocation to international stocks. Our most common recommendation is 15%. This is a little larger that the 10% found in the average large U.S. pension fund, but consistent with many other findings in the area of optimal asset allocation strategies. With small accounts, this exposure can be omitted until account balances reach $100,000 in total.

Emerging market exposure should be a minor proportion of the international allocation. It can be omitted completely or be from 10% to 30% of the total international stock allocation.

Value, Growth and Full Index
Many advisors are big fans of the full index, often by default rather than as a conscious choice. I like the value and full index classes the most and the growth asset class the least. There are times when growth is going full guns, and if you do not have some exposure to it in your mix, you feel left out of the gains. I recommend growth stocks only with large companies. An allocation to large U.S. growth stocks is essentially a defensive diversification strategy, not a return maximization strategy.

Some financial planners or individual investors will argue that a good small company active manager can substantially outperform with growth stocks. They will cite several "home run" stories to justify why you must use a manager that can find you the next home run. The research data does not support this as being possible on a consistent basis. In fact, the data suggests that true small-cap growth stock investing is betting on a substantially handicapped asset class to outperform. It could work in the short run but, over the long-term, but its odds for outperforming the basic full index are long at best.

Real Estate
Real estate is an excellent diversifier for large stocks. They work very well together. I recommend that your allocation to real estate be done as a portion of your large stocks. My suggested range is 30% to 70% of your large stock allocation. See the asset allocation tip in the real estate section for a more detailed suggestion.

Bonds
The stock to bond allocation is the best known asset allocation ratio. Here you will find wider agreement amongst advisors and large pension fund managers.

Large long-term pension managers who build moderate, balanced portfolios end up with a stock to bond allocation of

60% to 65% in stocks. A conservative long-term portfolio would have 50% in stocks and an aggressive portfolio would have 80% to 85% in stocks. Some investors may even have 100% in stocks, but this is an overly aggressive long-term approach in our opinion. If 40% of that were in real estate (50% of the large stock allocation) then the overall portfolio would perform more like an 85% stock portfolio.

The debate between advisors, with regard to bonds, has more to do with the term and quality, rather than with the allocation. Most advisors understand that it is much more efficient to get higher returns from stocks or real estate than it is from lengthening the term or reducing the quality of bonds. As such, I recommend you only use short term and high quality bonds in an asset allocation.

Portfolio Rebalancing
To maintain risk within stated levels, all portfolios need to be rebalanced. Rebalancing is an exercise that requires an approach devoid of emotion.

Most individual investors would add new money to the mutual fund that had produced the highest return in the last period. Further, they may even consider selling some of the funds that did not do well in the last period and buy more of what did do well.

Rebalancing strategy, on the other hand, uses new money to buy more of what has not recently performed well. It may also sell some of what has performed best and buy more of what has under performed.

Studies have shown that rebalancing once a year is optimal. I recommend that your portfolio be rebalanced when new contributions are made, and then once a year, if necessary.

Chapter 10 - Investment Considerations

The charts, graphs, tables and examples contained in this book are offered for purposes of illustration only. They do not imply the return that may be available on any particular investment.

Picking Winners in Advance

How a fund performs on a relative basis to other funds in the current year tells you nothing about how it will perform next year or over the next few years.

A Wall Street Journal article, dated Wednesday January 15, 2003, titled "*Mutual Fund Ratings Come Under Fire*", concluded that even Morningstar and Value Line rating services couldn't help much with predicting the better performing funds: "A new study concludes that mutual funds given high ratings by Morningstar and Value Line – both used by investors to choose among funds – don't necessarily do better than those with middling ratings." It also went on to say, "This is not the first study to point out that past performance is not a reliable measure of future results."

Morningstar Ratings

Morningstar does a superior job providing data about how individual mutual funds are structured. Recently Morningstar overhauled the star rating system to create more categories. The new categories now differentiate between value, growth and the full index for each major stock asset class. This gives the new star ratings more accuracy and gives the user better information.

The drawbacks to Morningstar's rating system, and all other present rating systems, is that the number of years being measured is very short. As we have said, even 25 years is a relatively short period for evaluating relative return relationships. Three to five year data is obviously very unreliable, but often the only information available.

Even with perfect backward measurement, no mutual fund rating system or magazine can reliably predict which mutual funds will be the top performers next year. It is simply impossible.

The Morningstar "star system", and others like it, are ineffective at helping you pick future top-performing funds. You will do better by picking index funds with low costs and low turnover ratios than by picking a fund with lots of stars.

Predicting Long Term Winners
I can tell you how to do this reliably! Over fifteen years, it is possible to know which funds will be amongst the top 20% of all funds in that asset class and style category. Funds that hold to their asset class (like an index fund) and have the lowest administration fees and portfolio turnover rates will be in the top 20% of all funds, in that asset class, after 15 years. It really is that easy.

Over long periods, active security selection and market timing decisions of fund managers will drag down performance.

Over the long term, the asset class you have invested in (U.S large stocks, U.S. small stocks, international large stocks, international small stocks, emerging markets, long term bonds, and short term bonds) is the most important determinant of return. The style weightings are next in importance, followed by sector weighting. Then finally, we get down to individual security selection and market timing decisions.

The best fund comparisons are those that compare funds on an equal basis as to asset class, style type and sector weightings. Consequently, what is being measured is purely the ability of a manager to add value. This will be based on their research, purchasing strategies, and their systems in choosing individual companies and timing of purchases and sales. Fund benchmark systems like Morningstar's have not yet attained this level of sophistication, but likely will in the future.

Market Timing Strategies
Market timing determines only 1.7% of the variance in return to a portfolio.
It can be a cost or a benefit, but market timing is always expensive because it costs money to buy and sell. The more you buy and sell the more it costs.

Historically, equities have had a negative return about 30% of the time; however, investors keep searching for a way to predict and then avoid the negative returns to compound their wealth faster and with less risk.

With the overwhelming evidence against market timing strategies over the long term, it takes a leap of faith to continue to use market-timing practices. If you are a trustee with fiduciary liabilities for a qualified plan (for example, a company 401(k) plan where you have employees in the retirement plan) it is a gambler's trap to not use active management.

Annual Fund Administration Fees
Fund administration fees are deducted by fund providers to cover costs associated with running the fund. These costs primarily consist of staff costs, overhead, printing, postage, marketing, and registering investments.

In addition to fund administration fees, a fund may also have 12B-1 fees. These are annual fees paid to a financial advisor. Only commission-earning financial advisors purchase funds with this cost added.

Some mutual funds have a front- and/or a back-end load. This is a percentage of the fund purchase price that is either paid to the financial advisor or broker as a sales charge.

Vanguard and other fund families have a front- or back-end load of 1.0% that does not go to a selling agent but instead goes to offset the fund's trading costs, and keep down portfolio turnover costs.

Each fund is required to disclose its annual administrative fees, 12B-1 fees and front- and back-end loads in their prospectus.

2002 Annual Fund Administration Fees

	Average Fund	Vanguard Index
U.S. Large Stocks	1.41%	0.18%
U.S. Small Stocks	1.63%	0.27%
REIT's	1.61%	0.28%
International Stocks	1.72%	0.64%
Bond Funds	0.98%	0.21%

Annual Turnover Costs

Portfolio turnover costs are the costs incurred when mutual funds buy and sell securities each year. Portfolio turnover costs are not a disclosed cost and are only reflected as reduced fund performance. Mutual funds must disclose the amount of portfolio turnover they have, so investors are informed of this hidden cost indirectly. This is expressed as the lower of purchase or sales for the year as a percent of total assets in the fund. Other things being equal, a mutual fund with higher turnover will produce lower returns.

2002 Annual Fund Turnover Percentage

	Average Fund	Vanguard Index
U.S. Large Stocks	95%	4%
U.S. Small Stocks	107%	39%
REIT's	58%	10%
International Stocks	102%	37%
Bond Funds	183%	135%

Source: Dimensional Fund Advisors

An efficient large U.S. stock fund has a transaction cost of 0.5% of the asset value. This means if the turnover percentage for that fund was 100% for the year, the return was reduced by 0.5% that year due to transaction costs of the turnover.

A typical small U.S. stock fund has a much higher transaction cost ranging from 1.5% to as much as 10.0% for the smallest companies. An average cost for a U.S. small stock would be around 4.0% of the asset value traded. The very largest traders in small stocks are able to do block trades that reduce this cost, on average, by 3% or more. The largest of these companies doing most of the block trades in small stocks can execute up to 90% of its trades as block trades. Thus, the volume of small stocks trades a firm undertakes is very important, as it lowers trading costs and gives the fund a cost advantage over the long term that is very substantial. Dimensional Fund Advisors (DFA) is the largest firm in the world that trades both U.S. and international small stocks and, hence, enjoys a unique small stock trading cost advantage.

Custodian Costs
Custodian costs are the costs incurred in having your investments held by a third party and to execute buy and sell orders through this custodian. Custodians are able to make settlements and to receive both annual dividends and interest payments electronically. Custodians also report monthly, quarterly or annually on your holdings.

Custodian costs are absorbed by most mutual funds when you invest directly and meet their minimum account balance requirements. Online brokerage firms and retail brokerage firms cover their custodian costs in the trade cost you pay per transaction.

When you use a financial planner, you will pay a trade cost to the custodian used by the financial planner. Schwab Institutional is the largest custodian for financial advisors. The biggest financial advisors get lower rates from Schwab than do smaller advisors.

Index Funds - Cost Advantage

The track record for mutual funds is that, over the long term, they tend to under perform the stock market by the amount of their fees and their transaction costs.

Think of the stock market as a pie with a 10% return. To obtain their share of the 10% pie, investors pay fees. For a retail or conventional mutual fund, these costs (administration fees and portfolio investment costs) are about 2% a year, leaving a net return of 8%.

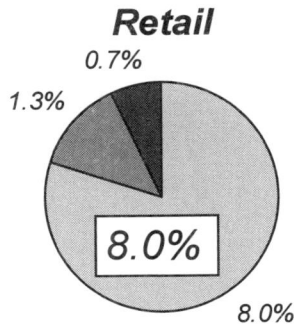

Retail

0.7%

1.3%

8.0%

8.0%

For an institutional fund, the costs are only 0.3% a year, leaving a return of 9.7%.

Institutional

0.1%

0.2%

9.7%

9.7%

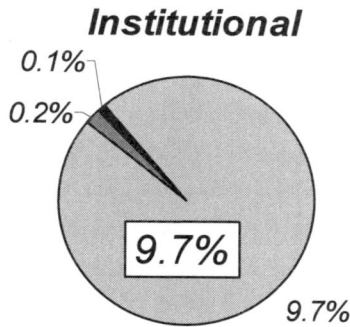

The question investors have to ask themselves is - will an active manager or actively managed fund be able to make up their higher fees and higher transactions costs?

Indexing, or statistical investing, is a strategy that, in the short run, will outperform 40% to 70% of all funds within that asset class – and over the long haul will outperform nearly all funds within that asset class. Institutional and individual investors increasingly use passive investment approaches.

Institutional Mutual Funds
There are two main types of mutual funds, those available to retail customers and those only available to the largest accounts – institutional funds. Institutional funds are held by large pension funds and are now available through some financial planners.

Institutional investors with large portfolios to invest, together with some financial planners, demand and receive lower fees and lower turnover rates due to being long-term investors.

Vanguard offers both retail and institutional shares, as do many other fund providers. Vanguard's retail index funds are often as low or lower in cost as other mutual fund family's institutional products.

Mutual Funds - Individual Securities – Exchange Traded Funds (ETF's)

Mutual funds are generally preferable to individual purchases in building your investment core. The benefits of using mutual funds are substantial. They allow for a wide diversification with a small investment, and due to their size, the managers of mutual funds can purchase and sell securities at a lower cost than individuals can.

Mutual funds often employ significant discipline to the investment process, more than an individual would be able to duplicate. The managers of mutual funds do an excellent job of administering the investment holdings and they provide timely and complete reporting. Before buying or selling securities, managers of mutual funds do extensive research; and some index mutual fund managers take advantage of their size by developing sophisticated buy and sell strategies to maximize the after-fee returns to the fund in a way that trust or individual investors could not duplicate.

Exchange Traded Funds (ETFs) are a viable alternative to mutual funds. This is a new class of investment that is growing very rapidly and comprises a basket of securities that are traded like stocks rather than mutual funds. These are index funds. ETFs are able to be sector specific, not just asset class specific. This means you can buy very specific industry plays with ETFs that are not available in mutual funds. ETFs can be bought and sold during the trading day (like a stock), not at the end of a trading day like a mutual fund. ETFs are tax efficient in that you own the underlying asset, not just a share in a mutual fund. Thus, the only time you pay taxes is when you actually sell.

ETFs have very low fund costs as compared to most mutual funds and are even slightly below the cost of owning a Vanguard index mutual fund. This benefit, however, is often overstated. For when you sell most ETFs, you are given a basket of actual stocks that must be traded. There is a cost involved in this trade which adds to the real cost of ownership. Morningstar has estimated that it takes a two-year holding period for an ETF to have a cost structure comparable to a Vanguard index mutual fund.

The tax advantage of ETFs is often overstated as well. My overall conclusion is that ETFs are an excellent investment alternative for most asset class holdings where you plan to buy and hold. The tax advantage of ETF's make their use in taxable accounts most attractive.

The biggest ETFs traded today are the Qubes (QQQ), with an average daily volume of 71 million shares, according to Morningstar in May 2003. The second trading volume contender is from a group of ETFs called SPDRs (spiders) made up of the S&P 500 and various subsets of the S&P 500. Their daily volume, according to Morningstar in May 2003, is 39 million shares a day.

Some other ETFs include Diamonds (which track the DJIA), IShares marketed by Barclays Global Investors, StreeTracks by State Street Global Advisors (covering various indexes), VIPERs (Vanguard's various ETF offerings), and HOLDRs from Merrill Lynch.

Retail Mutual Funds A, B & C Shares
In 2003 some mutual funds received a black eye for practices that were found to be unethical to the shareholders. Brokers were found guilty of putting customers into more expensive and inappropriate classes of mutual funds for their own profit.

One of these practices was found in the escalation of the 12B-1 fees in class A, B and C shares. These are fees levied each year by the fund and paid to the advisor, and fees paid for redemptions in the first eight years. Historically, these were only 0.25% a year. Recently some advisors and large brokerage firms have raised these fees.

"A" shares charges an upfront commission that can be as much as 5.75% plus a small 12B-1 fee of 0.25% a year.

"B" shares do not charge an initial brokerage commission but charge a 12B-1 fee of about 1% a year initially declining to 0.25%

over time. Also, if investors sell these shares within six years of purchase they must pay a back end commission as well. This class of shares was most commonly found to have abuses in recent NASD reviews.

"C" shares are similar to "B" shares in that they do not have an upfront fee. The 12B-1 fee is 1% but unlike B shares it never declines. After the first year there is no back end commission on the sale of these funds.

For most funds there are no-load options also available that completely avoid the potential for abusive advisor fees. What is most disturbing about these fees is they are for the most part very difficult for the investor to see as they are levied by the fund. This opened the door for excessive charges in comparison to the services being provided.

Active versus Passive

Retail or institutional mutual funds break down into two main types; those actively managed and those passively managed. ETFs are always passively managed.

Although the data and research has been overwhelmingly consistent regarding this matter for years, the majority of investors still choose active managers to implement their investment programs. They, presumably, hope the active funds they choose will be one of the few superior performing actively managed funds over the long term. Some individual investors expect to own only winners all of the time. Whenever they get a less than positive result, they begin to second guess themselves. This belief is simply not realistic and will be detrimental to your wealth, until you accept the facts.

Active Management

Actively managed funds are those where the manager chooses the companies to hold in the fund and the timing of when to buy and sell those companies. For decades, this was the dominant form of portfolio management and mutual fund available to the individual investor.

The premise of active management is that your manager knows how to outperform the market over time, and after his fees and costs his net return will be better than the market or the appropriate benchmark index fund.

The active fund manager also promises that he or she knows when it is a good time to buy or sell a company. Most active management is based on visiting hundreds of prospective companies. This makes for a good story but the hard facts show it does not reliably produce better performance over the long term.

Security selection determines only 4.6% of the total return (Brinson, Beebower, Hood *et al.*, 1991). The chance, therefore, that an active manager can add additional value over time, net of fees, is remote. If the investment approach is not consistently applied, the manager is practicing market timing, and most managers who practice security selection employ some degree of market timing.

Passively Managed Funds
ETFs, index or statistically managed funds define a statistical universe of assets to hold. The fund then buys and holds the entire universe, or holds a group of stocks that represents that universe. Most index funds weight their holdings on a market capitalization basis (relative value).

Example: if the value of all Microsoft outstanding shares is 1% of the value of all S&P 500 stocks, the index fund for the S&P 500 will hold 1% of its value in Microsoft stock.

Index investing is not limited to the full representation of a class of assets. Based on the Fama-French data from the last 77 years, it is possible to use high book-to-market indexing to improve the S&P 500 returns by 2% a year on average. Index (statistical) investing represents the best long-term method of investing for the core of the investment stock portfolio.

When to Use Active Funds - Index Funds – ETFs

Use Index Funds or ETFs for:

All stock funds in the value category
Large U.S. & international stocks – full index
Bond funds

Use Index Funds, ETFs or Active Management for:
Large U.S. & international stocks - growth
Small U.S. & International stocks - full index
Large emerging market stocks – full index
Small emerging market stocks – full index

Use Active Management only for:
Large emerging markets stocks - growth
Small U.S. & international stocks – growth (not recommended)

Chapter 11 - Investment Advisory Services

The examples and graphs provided in this chapter are for purposes of illustration only and do not imply the return that may be available on any particular investment.

As a reminder, Healthy Wealth does not offer investment advisory services. The information in this chapter about investment / financial advisors is given for educational purposes and not to sell a service. I have been a fe based financial advisor and this knowledge was learned first hand working in the business.

I believe that most of you will do better working with a financial advisor rather than working on your own.

Financial Planner & Investment Advisor Services
Investment advisors perform a variety of functions:

- Help you select an appropriate portfolio design that is well balanced and not too aggressive for your chosen risk tolerance and time horizon
- Support you in maintaining a long-term approach to investing
- Help you set and monitor your performance according to a savings plan
- Develop and annually maintain your financial plan
- Establish and maintain a written investment policy

- Provide ongoing education about investing
- Report annual performance
- Answer your investment questions
- Evaluate new investment research for you
- Help select appropriate investment funds to implement your plan
- Help select individual stocks to implement your investment plan
- Help you invest in real estate
- Recommend good real estate managers
- Advise you on banking matters
- Leverage their aggregated buying power to provide investment cost savings
- Estate planning design, and referrals to a good attorney
- Tax strategies associated with your investing and financial planning
- Business management advice
- Pension plan design and documents
- Corporate document assistance
- Trust advice

Investment advisors' fees vary depending upon the services they provide and the number of intermediaries involved. These fees are usually reduced as the managed assets increase. A typical fee is 1% of assets under management for stocks and bonds.

When to Go it Alone

First, let me qualify this. I believe every investor should have financial advisors. The amount of advice you use will depend on your expertise in each of the following areas.

Even the best athletes have regular coaches to help them get better or discover weaknesses. Naturally, when you are developing, you need more help than when you are experienced. As you begin to succeed, you can cut back, but not totally eliminate your need for professional advice.

Check the following questions:
- Are you a do-it-yourselfer in many aspects of your life?
- Do you consider your investment intelligence to be high? Do you know how to create a well diversified portfolio

design? Do you know the difference between value and growth stocks? Do you understand terms like market capitalization?

- Do you have real experience with staying with under performing funds for many years until they recover?
- Have you the discipline to add money to a mutual fund that declined 25% in the previous year, when the other funds all made a profit, because this is what must be done to rebalance your portfolio?
- Do you have good self-discipline and a track record of writing out a portfolio design strategy, and staying with that design when markets are down?
- Are you already proficient as a real estate investor?

If you can answer yes to the questions above then you are a good candidate to invest on your own. Otherwise, a financial advisor is your fastest path to financial independence even after paying 1.0% a year.

Investment technology is dynamic and changing, new research is evolving every year. New fund choices, new risk dimensions, and new asset classes are constantly evolving. Do you have the time and training to keep up with, and stay on top of, these changes?

Statistical research demonstrates that individual investors significantly under perform in the market.

When do individuals decide to buy a mutual fund? After it has been doing well, and it looks like a good fund. What happens after they buy into the fund? In all likelihood, it under-performs in the next few years.

What do individual investors do when they expect a 90th percentile performance but get only 20th? They sell. However, was that the right thing to do?

Perhaps the most significant benefit of using an investment advisor is that, through their systems and support, you will behave more like a successful long-term investor – at the times when it matters most.

114

Not all financial advisors are asset class investors. Some believe they can best attract clients, and create the most value added, by finding funds with the best track record. Be aware this approach may sound like the Promised Land, but it is engineered to under-perform over the long term.

Investment Advisor Fees

The way a firm derives its fees from you is important. The philosophy of a firm is in large part influenced by their fee and income structure. The following is a brief summary of the basic types.

Fee Only® (a registered trademark of NAPFA) Advisor

Here the advisory firm is paid their fees based on either assets under management, retainers, or hourly or project fees. This approach comes with the least amount of conflict of interest. This sector of advisors is my personal choice. The drawback is that these types of advisors can often be mediocre in their people and business skills. Thus, they can come up short when it comes to systemizing their business and your interaction. They also may not be as strong as you might need them to be in a crisis. The solution is for you to be determined to find a *good* advisor of this type.

There are two different types of Fee Only advisors. The first has less conflict of interest because they do not sell or recommend any product offered by their own firm. The second is typically found with large brokerage firms. Their financial planners are paid a salary based on their assets under management, but the parent company makes more money when you use their products. Somewhere in the reward system of these firms, the advisors are rewarded for recommending and getting you to invest in their products.

Fee Based Advisor

Although the name sounds confusingly like Fee Only advisors, there is an important difference. Fee Based advisors also charge commissions. Almost all insurance products are sold to individuals under a commission arrangement. Some Fee Based Advisors charge asset management fees for their investment services, and then commissions for insurance sales. This is a very healthy situation, and really as good as a Fee Only relationship as long as the investment philosophy is index, asset class or ETF based.

Other fee based advisors get part of their fees from mutual fund loads or from transaction fees on the purchase and sale of stocks and bonds. Mutual fund loads come in two forms, an up front or exit load and an annual 12B-1 fee paid to the fund advisor by the mutual fund. This form of compensation is most common with smaller accounts.

Fee Based and Commission Offsetting Advisor
Typically, this arrangement is found with an advisor that uses both loaded and load free investments. For the smaller investor this is a fair way to pay for services.

Annual Asset Management Fees plus Negotiated Commissions on Trades
This fee structure is common with the large brokerage houses today. I believe this is a better arrangement for investors than a straight commission arrangement as previously offered by brokerage houses. I am opposed to this system when a broker can negotiate rates with you. Often the advisor has a range of fee rates he/she can charge, and you only get offered the lowest rate after comparing information from friends who use the same firm.

I find something inherently wrong with a system that tries to take advantage of you. Can you really trust a financial advisor after you learn they were not being up front with you about your fee arrangement?

Wrap Fee Program
This is where you pay a flat fee from 1% to 4% a year for all of the costs associated with your investment account. It usually covers the financial advisor's fee, the fund management fees, the account custodian fees, and any trading costs. These fees are often negotiable and require you to do your homework and bargain with the advisor.

Some wrap programs are there to simplify the process for small advisors. Some of them promote market timing and other difficult-to-fulfill promises. To know if these programs are right for you, look into the details of the program.

I find this kind of program is best for a small to medium size client working with a small advisor who has the oversight of a large provider. These large providers can be sharks or dolphins, you just have to do your homework to figure out which category they belong to before turning over your money.

Finding a Financial Planner
Using a financial planner is one of the best investments you can make in order to reach financial independence. They have an array of systems to offer you. These systems make it easier for you to take the steps necessary to make real progress and avoid major setbacks.

Financial planners typically charge their clients a percentage of the assets they manage. For stocks and bonds, this percentage starts at around 1.0% a year and reduces for higher balances to around 0.5% a year. For real estate, this fee often does not exist, and when it does, it is typically 0.5% of the net worth of the real estate.

Financial planners may offer other services like estate planning, family financial education, income tax planning and preparation, pension plan design and documentation, business consulting, insurance evaluations, practice transition consulting, corporate documentation, real estate consulting, real estate brokerage, real estate management, bill paying, and similar services. Some of these services are included in the investment fee and some are additional.

Finding the right financial planner is even more important than finding the right CPA. Here are some tips on finding the right planner for you:

- Ask your successful friends and colleagues who they use.

- Your CPA may be a good financial advisor alternative if they have developed this speciality and have the experience.

- Industry referral sources. NAPFA is the national association of fee only financial advisors. They provide a list of referrals that are all carefully screened to be Fee Only in all aspects of their business. Unfortunately, they will eliminate anyone who also provides real estate brokerage or business transition services for a commission. They can be found at http://napfa.org.

  The main organization for financial advisors is called the Financial Planners Association. They have over 5,000 certified financial planners as members and they provide referrals. The FPA can be found at http://fpanet.org.

If your interest lies more in an occasional question or financial plan there is another group of hourly based financial planners called Garrett Planning Network http://garrettplanningnetwork.com. They have approximately 120 financial planners in their network who charge by the hour.

Other sources, like Charles Schwab & Co., also make referrals. Charles Schwab and some of the other large industry players receive a commission for these referrals. I recommend you stay away from these industry-based referral sources.

Here is what to do once you get a short list of advisors to interview:

- Request brochures and any other information they can provide to help you understand their services.

- Interview at least three planners.

- Discuss their fee approach. Keep asking questions until you understand.

- What is the investment philosophy of the firm? This is the most important question you will ask. Make sure you understand where they stand on active versus passive management, market timing philosophies, the typical mutual funds they recommend and why, value and growth, international stocks, and, of course, real estate.

- Ask about their financial planning process. What software do they use? How often do they update your plan. How do they charge for a plan?

- Ask about real estate. Do they recommend or counsel you on direct real estate investing as well as REITs. Ask what would be a typical real estate allocation for a client of theirs today. Ask what other professionals they work with to help with real estate investing. This answer will be very telling. If they have a well defined program around real estate, this list will be long, either with internal staff or external consultants. If they have no external specialists, take any claims that they do direct real estate consulting with a grain of salt.

- Finding a financial advisor who includes direct real estate investing can be challenging. You may find it preferable to get one advisor for stocks, bonds, and REITs, and another for direct real estate investing. If you do this, it is important to make sure your stock, bond and REIT advisor is "direct real estate investing friendly". Sometimes they will want you to sell your real estate so they can put the proceeds into stocks, bonds and REITs, because that is what they get paid for.

- Ask how they charge for real estate support services. A firm with a separate fee structure for this service means they really do this work.

- How much money do they have under advisement?

- How many clients do they have in your same industry? You want someone who knows the issues you and your profession have to deal with.

- How many financial planners are on staff? Having more than one is important. A successful philosophy and practice usually attracts other top professionals.

- Ask how many clients the planners in this firm typically work with.

- Where are their office(s)?

How to Order More Books from Healthy Wealth
The first place to go is the http://healthywealth.com website for the latest information and order forms. We offer free shipping for orders placed on the Healthy Wealth website.

Two other books are planned for release in 2004 or early 2005.
Money Basics – For the Young Adult
Families and Money - The Entitlement Trap

More Information Now From Healthy Wealth
Healthy Wealth has articles it has published and articles by others available on its website, http://healthywealth.com. It also has topic based Questions and Answers.

Let Me Know How I Can Improve
Send me an email and let me know any thought or ideas you have about this book and how I can make it better for you next time. You can address your email to don@healthywealth.com.

Unfortunately I cannot respond to your email questions. Thank you for your understanding in advance.

Index

Symbols

B

C

D

E

F

G

H

I

Ian Rowley 68
Ibbotson-Sinquefield 39
IRA 13, 59, 92
IShares 108

J

John R. Chisolm 68
Journal of Financial Analysis *54*

M

Mercer Global Advisors 6
Merrill Lynch 108
MGA 24, 33
Morningstar 7, 18, 44, 63, 82, 96, 101, 102, 108

N

NAPFA 115, 118
NASDAQ 1000 96

P

Pay Yourself First 21, 22, 31, 85
Professor Eugene Fama 61
Professor Kenneth French 61, 69
Professor Markowitz 50, 54
Professor Merton Miller 51
Professor Sharpe 50
Professor William Sharpe 61, 68
Prudent Investor Rule 82

R

REIT 58, 78, 80, 82, 84, 92, 94, 119
Roger Ibbotson and Paul Kaplan 42

S

Schwab 2000 95
Size and Book-to-Market Equity 61
State Street Global Advisors 108
StreeTracks 108

T

The Entitlement Trap 26, 27, 120
Three factor model 61
three factor model 62

This page intentionally left blank

This page intentionally left blank

This page intentionally left blank

This page intentionally left blank

To Order More Books

Healthy Wealth

	Each	Amount	Total
Successful Investing	$16.95	_____	_____

Sales Tax (Your local Rate) _____% _____
   Your 5 digit Zip code _____

Shipping - Free Media Mail Shipping

Total $ _____

Send check and copy of order form to:

   Don Chambers
   Healthy Wealth
   3945 South Wasatch Blvd. #247
   Salt Lake City, UT 84124

Or go to websites: http://healthywealth.com
                    (free shipping, requires PayPal)

                    http://amazon.com
                    (credit card purchases)